DUDE,
YOU'RE GETTING
MARRIED!

DUDE,
YOU'RE GETTING
MARRIED!

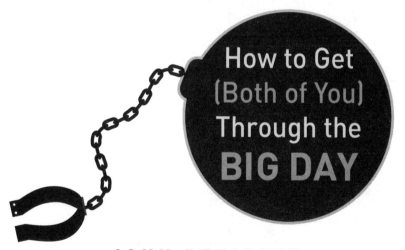

How to Get
(Both of You)
Through the
BIG DAY

JOHN PFEIFFER

Author of the bestselling *Dude, You're Gonna Be a Dad!*

A **adams**media
Avon, Massachusetts

Published by
Adams Media, a division of F+W Media, Inc.
57 Littlefield Street, Avon, MA 02322. U.S.A.
www.adamsmedia.com

Contains material adapted and abridged from *The Everything® Wedding Organizer, 3rd
Edition*, by Shelly Hagen, copyright © 2012, 2006, 1998 by F+W Media, Inc., ISBN 10:
1-4405-2686-9, ISBN 13: 978-1-4405-2686-2.

ISBN 10: 1-4405-6228-8
ISBN 13: 978-1-4405-6228-0
eISBN 10: 1-4405-6229-6
eISBN 13: 978-1-4405-6229-7

Printed in the United States of America.

10 9 8 7 6 5 4 3 2 1

Library of Congress Cataloging-in-Publication Data

Pfeiffer, John.
  Dude, you're getting married! / John Pfeiffer.
    pages cm
  Includes index.
  ISBN-13: 978-1-4405-6228-0 (pbk.)
  ISBN-10: 1-4405-6228-8 (pbk.)
  ISBN-13: 978-1-4405-6229-7 (ebook)
  ISBN-10: 1-4405-6229-6 (ebook)
1. Wedding etiquette. 2. Bridegrooms. 3. Weddings--Planning. 4. Etiquette for
men. I. Title.
  BJ2051.P48 2013
  395.2'2--dc23
                                2013030924

This publication is designed to provide accurate and authoritative information with regard to
the subject matter covered. It is sold with the understanding that the publisher is not engaged
in rendering legal, accounting, or other professional advice. If legal advice or other expert
assistance is required, the services of a competent professional person should be sought.
  —From a *Declaration of Principles* jointly adopted by a Committee of the American Bar
            Association and a Committee of Publishers and Associations

Many of the designations used by manufacturers and sellers to distinguish their product are
claimed as trademarks. Where those designations appear in this book and F+W Media was
aware of a trademark claim, the designations have been printed with initial capital letters.

This book is available at quantity discounts for bulk purchases.
For information, please call 1-800-289-0963.

To Alana, with love . . .

Acknowledgments

A special thanks to everyone at Adams that I work with (Katie, Beth, and Brendan) and all of the hard-working folks that I don't get to meet. Thanks for doing your best to prop up my words. A very special thank you to the very dynamic duo of Jennifer and Dawn at The Funky Shack (*www.funkyshackweddings.com*). Besides being talented, you are also passionate about what you do. Many thanks for the time and information.

CONTENTS

Introduction

You will never forget the first time you met her. She had that "je ne sais quoi" that caught your eye. She was your perfect counterpoint, the yin to your yang. Heck, you knew from the moment you saw her that she "completed" you. You two just knew it was love at first sight. You had a whirlwind courtship, full of good times. Getting to know her just seemed to get better every day. You kept waiting for there to be some letdown or awful surprise—but it never came. And now you have decided that you simply cannot live without this special person in your life. So what happens next? How do you pop the question? How can you help your bride-to-be—known from now on as the BTB (easier to remember that way)—make it through the wedding planning process without losing her mind? How can you keep from losing yours? This is where *Dude, You're Getting Married!* comes into play.

You see, planning a wedding is, in and of itself, a fascinating thing. It's one part storybook, one part advanced budgeting, and one part logistics, all with a magical touch of interpersonal relations thrown in for good measure. Not only do you need to honor what is important to you; you, of course, need to take your soon-to-be spouse's opinion into consideration, as well—honoring family and religious traditions if they exist. This book will seek to help you successfully navigate this jungle.

And because nobody enters into this sacred union (I hope) with anything less than the utmost optimism and excitement, you want to do it the right way. But what is the right way? How should the two of you get started on this wonderful journey together? Well, the real answer is that any way the two of you agree to get married will be just fine. If it is right for both of you, who is to say you are wrong? It's your lives, after all. But what we will do here is go through many of the rules and traditions of getting married, and discuss how you can play your role to the fullest. So pick out that ring, rent that tux, figure out those seating charts, and start being an active and engaged fiancé who will get (both of you) to the church on time!

CHAPTER I

Popping the Question

So you've made up your mind! After much consideration (I hope), your heart and mind are in agreement; you've decided that you're ready to pledge your everlasting love to that someone special; and you're going to put yourself on the line and pop the question. Well, congratulations! Finding that one special woman is the hard part. And, let's be honest, you probably have a pretty good idea that she's going to say yes before you decide to start throwing around marriage proposals. But still, you want the proposal—and everything that goes along with it—to be special. So, let's look at a few things that you should be thinking about to make the proposal just right.

Pre-Proposal Considerations

Before you actually pop the question, sit down and take the time to think through a few things. Are you guys at the right stage of your relationship to tie the knot, or did you just meet last week? Or a few minutes ago at the craps table?

Are *you* convinced that this girl is The One? Yes! Okay. Just checking. Now that we've got that covered, since getting married is something that everyone will look back on and your friends will talk about, you probably want things to be perfect. You want to do this right, from the proposal all the way through to the ceremony and beyond. For many men, the first step in this process is asking her parents' permission for their daughter's hand in marriage. Now, this may seem slightly old-fashioned, but it can also be a timeless and classic step. But how do you bring it up? How do you know if it's even the right thing to do? Well . . .

> *Love is friendship set on fire.*
> *—Jeremy Taylor, author*

Know Your Bride

We've gotten to the gray area where it's important to "Know Your Bride." Picture someone saying this in a big, booming game show voice. But seriously, ask yourself if your soon-to-be fiancée will feel that her heart is hers and hers alone to give away and that asking her parents for her hand in marriage is sexist and old-fashioned. If so, then *maybe* talking to her mom and dad isn't the path for you. If this is the case, after you pop the question maybe the two of you can go to her parents together and ask permission. At that point it will be more ceremonial than anything, but it's still a nice gesture. Besides, it will give you some extra credit when you start taking "In-Law 101," otherwise known as the rest of the wedding planning (and the rest of your life).

Talk to Mom and Dad

If you have made the decision to ask the parents' permission, then bully for you. In my humble opinion, it is a nice start to the potentially long-lasting relationship with your father-in-law. Unless there have been major issues in the history between you and the family, this is hopefully going to be a mostly ceremonial exercise. You ask permission and your BTB's dad gives you a few words of wisdom and then tells you to go ahead with his blessing. In some sense, you are giving respect to him by asking and letting him know what's coming.

So that's it at a high level. But what about the actual execution of the thing? First, it will depend on where the parents are located. If they are on a planet far, far away, you will most likely just make a phone call. Make sure you politely ask if Dad has a few minutes to talk before you get into it. Nothing worse than an old man cutting you off in conversation because he is in a rush to eat his meatloaf. Then, once you know he has some time, gently get into it.

If the BTB's parents are right around the corner, you will want to approach the situation differently. You can choose how to proceed based on your impression of them, but to me the correct play is to talk to Mom and Dad together. We know Dad played his part, but Mom did give birth after all and she deserves to be in the loop. Perhaps you could have dinner with them, or take a few minutes to grab lunch during the workday. Yes, they will know something's up, but hopefully in a good way.

So what happens next? I hope for everyone involved their answer is a resounding "Yes!" and they decide to pick up the bill for the lunch, with hugs and handshakes for everyone. But even though it is somewhat of a formality, what if they say "No"? If your relationship has had some issues, then you must at least know this is a possibility. Then the ball is in your court on what to do next, and you are in a difficult position. Think hard about what you do next. If you move forward with the proposal, just realize Thanksgiving dinner could be a little awkward.

Now, if you have done some scenario planning and decided it is not worth it to ask permission, then keep everything you've read in mind and keep on moving forward. Good luck!

Okay, you've either talked to your future fiancée's parents—or not—and now it's time to move onwards and upwards on your path toward wedded bliss. Of course, I'm talking about buying the engagement ring . . .

For Your Fiancée

However you decide to approach the permissions issue, be sure to think it through and figure out what your soon-to-be fiancée wants before you move forward. Start a hypothetical discussion about the subject of asking the parents' permission first when watching the latest romantic comedy entitled *Beautiful Girl with a Heart of Gold Who Can't Find Love*. It stars Kate Hudson! (Just kidding—but someone should make this movie.) Or maybe you can broach the subject when a friend gets engaged. Even if one of the "trending now" topics is Justin Bieber's engagement, don't pass up the opportunity to gather intel on what your future bride may want. Since you won't be asking for a while, it will make her wonder just what exactly is going on in your head. The further out you can begin your guerrilla campaign, the better. ■

The Ring

Have you bought the ring? In my mind, the ring is an important symbol of your love. It will also be something her friends will look at right away—and some of them will judge you, for better or for worse.

What Kind of Ring Will You Get?

So far we have assumed you are going out on your own to make this life-changing purchase. If that's the case, then know your bride (KYB from here on out). Does she tend to wear small, understated jewelry? Or does she tend to go bolder, or more artistic? Some guys simply pop the question and then take her ring shopping. You creative types may want to use a family heirloom or a ring passed down to you from your family, which can be a wonderful option as it gives more meaning to the ring. Just allow for the fact that the style may not be exactly what your bride likes, and allow for the possibility she will want to use just the stone, or add to it. But let's take a look at our options, starting with the traditional diamond ring.

Diamonds Are a Girl's Best Friend

Before you go diamond shopping, you have some research to do. Be sure to know the following before you make your decision:

- **The Cs:** You will quickly be exposed to the classic "four Cs" of buying a diamond: Cut, Color, Clarity, Carat. Per their website, the GIA, or Gemological Institute of America, established the "4Cs" method for evaluating precious stones. The highlights of each category are as follows:

- *Cut:* The cut is the factor that affects the diamond's shine, sparkle, and brilliance. This is not describing the actual shape of the diamond as you would first think. It determines the diamond's proportions, symmetry, and polish, all of which affects the stone's ability to capture and reflect light. The better the score, the more perfect and symmetrical the stone.
- *Color:* When it comes to rating the color of a diamond, what is actually being scored is a *lack* of color. The closer the stone is to being colorless, the greater its value, and its score. The scoring goes from "D," which is the highest grade, to "Z," which the scale calls "Light" color, but is really the bottom score. Most of what you will see in a reputable store will be colorless or very close to it. If two stones' scores are very close on the scale, there is good chance your eye will not be able to tell the difference.
- *Clarity:* Diamonds are made deep inside Mother Earth. They are under a lot of pressure for long periods of time while being formed. The end result of this often leaves imperfections in the stone. They can be internal (inclusions) or external (blemishes). The scale goes from FL (flawless) to I3 (visible imperfections). There are eleven grades in all. You will not be purchasing a flawless diamond, as they are so rare most jewelers have never even seen one.

- *Carat:* Diamonds and gemstones are weighed in metric carats. Wait, isn't it *karat*, like 18-karat gold? Nope. The term *karat* refers to the purity of the gold. *Carat* is strictly a measure of weight. For us backwards Americans, that's about 0.2 grams per carat, approximately the weight of a paperclip. There is no fancy scale here; the bigger the diamond, the more carats it will weigh. This is the one "C" that the eye will be able to visibly distinguish. You may not be able to see small inclusions, but you will be able to tell the difference between a half carat and a full carat. So although you don't want a big yellow diamond, the size of the stone is the most visible sign of the value of the diamond.

- **Conflict-Free?:** You may be at the stage where you are saying: "Hey, I heard Kanye rap about conflict diamonds, what are those?" Or maybe you march against them in protest. But for those who do not know, conflict diamonds refer to diamonds that are illegally traded to fund wars. This often refers to the conflicts in war-torn areas like west and central Africa. They are also called "blood diamonds." Today, because of efforts by the United Nations, more than 99 percent of diamonds are now conflict-free, or from areas where the proceeds are not used to fund violence.

Nuptial Knowledge

How did the tradition of buying a diamond engagement ring come about?

■ There are varying opinions on the subject. Some say that in the early twentieth century the jewelry company De Beers launched a campaign to present the diamond as a rare gem reserved for only the most special occasions. We fell for it, hook, line, and sinker. Further research shows that even in the early twentieth century some couples got the honeymoon started a little early. Women took the expensive ring as a sign that their men were serious about going through with the marriage, and if the man backed out, the woman would have the ring to take with her.

Diamond Optional

So, do you really know your BTB? I mean, really *really* know her? Because if you take a swing and miss on this next call, you will find yourself in a difficult situation. I am referring to the growing trend of wedding rings that do not contain a diamond, and often use an alternate stone. It really does make a lot of sense. Who wouldn't be dazzled by a beautiful emerald or sapphire? Who would snicker if you decide to use her grandmother's pearl as the centerpiece of the ring? Besides, these stones are not so "spendy," if you will. These alternative stones can be extremely beautiful and unique—just make sure your BTB didn't have her heart set on a diamond ring.

So what are your options?

- **Pearl:** There seem to be two schools of thought on this option. The pros are that it makes for a classy and unique look, and it almost guarantees nobody will have a ring like it. The downside is that pearls are not very durable, and you are likely to have to replace the centerpiece every, say, five to eight years. Pearls are also very sensitive to chemicals, perfumes, and even soaps. She will really have to take this thing on and off frequently.

- **Sapphire:** The main thing I can discover concerning the downside of having a sapphire ring is that its color is so far from tradition. Many people may get confused about whether it is even an engagement ring at all.
- **Emerald:** This is another "soft" stone. I mean, it's not like I want to be punched in the face by someone sporting a fistful of emerald rings. But when the emeralds are exposed to daily wear and tear, bumping against door frames and desks, then they can get damaged.
- **Birthstone:** Birthstones are only a great idea if your BTB is really into it. It mostly screams of something for a necklace or other piece of complementary jewelry. Unless, of course, your BTB's month of birth is April. April's birthstone is . . . drumroll please . . . the diamond!

That is the summary of some of the most popular options. The main point here is that you want something beautiful and worthy of your BTB. You will want to do some sneaking around in advance: Ask her friends and parents, drop hints, anything you can think of to increase your knowledge of what kind of engagement ring she likes. I totally took a shot in the dark, and to this day my wife gets compliments and says, "John picked it out himself." I think she is still shocked.

History Repeating

If you have heard from every source imaginable that your soon-to-be BTB wants to incorporate her great-grandmother's stone or other family treasure, then act accordingly. You may have to give her an empty box and then the two of you can take the stone and go shopping for a setting to match.

Choose the Setting

The setting of the ring itself offers a whole other set of choices. White gold and traditional yellow gold are always stunning. If she requires a hypoallergenic metal, that's no problem—platinum will solve this issue. Platinum is the most expensive metal because of this property and the fact that it is built to last a lifetime. The important thing here is not just to make your BTB happy, but to make her overwhelmed! So dig deep and go that extra mile for her, and the extra dollars you put into the ring will be worth every penny when you see the look on her face. You will know in the first millisecond if you did a good job.

Set a Budget

There is a ring for every budget, and a ring to break every budget. Make the budget when you are thinking clearly. Then stick to it. It is easy for you to go into that store and get carried away. Your feeling of love for your BTB will carry you well beyond your original calculated cost. "Nothing is too good for my girl!" This thought will be in your head as you casually add another zero to the total cost of your purchase. While I do advocate digging deep and not scrimping on this particular purchase, you do not want to show up for the proposal dinner on a bicycle because you sold your car just to get the ring! When it comes to creating a ring budget, put a lot of thought into it. Then there is "'do' or 'do not'; there is no 'try.'" Take that little tidbit from Yoda ring shopping with you. When you are making out your budget, there are a few things to remember:

- **Keep It Challenging, but Realistic:** Just like your goals in other areas of life, your budget for the engagement ring should challenge you a bit without breaking the bank. You need to know what is realistic for your wallet *before* you go shopping, because those clever salespeople will "help" you into a bigger, more expensive ring in no time!
- **Stick with Tradition:** Traditionally, the price of the engagement ring should equal three months' salary. Also, one number floating out there says the average engagement ring costs just north of $5,000. But as you will discover, many of the "right" answers and traditions out there were created by other people and may not be right for you. So do your homework. Traditions are there for a reason. It's because somewhere along the way someone figured out the best way to handle the situation you are in right now. It doesn't mean it is the only way to do things, but traditions are usually tried-and-true. Then make sure it lines up with what your BTB wants. All of this is for her in many ways. So if she doesn't like it, then it isn't right.
- **Know That You're Buying More Than One:** You probably know this, but you are not actually just buying one ring. There is the engagement ring, the one you give her when you propose, and that's great. But in addition— if all goes well—you will be picking out a wedding band for your BTB, as well as a band for yourself. Depending

on what you decide to buy, the engagement ring may eat up a disproportionate amount of your total budget, but unless you are thinking of sporting some string on your finger, leave a few dollars for yourself.

Okay, now that you have crunched the numbers for the budget, and played detective and tried to pry the information out of her, there was one more thing you needed to do. What was that? Oh, that's right! It's time to propose!

How to Do It

You know, pop the question. As Paul Simon says, there are at least "50 Ways to Leave Your Lover," but there are even more fun and creative ways to ask her to marry you. As for me, I always favor something overly complex and dramatic. But that may not be your personal style. Here are some tried-and-true methods, but remember, no proposal is guaranteed. And guys, if you have any useful information like her favorite proposal scene from a movie, or a romantic tie in to something special between the two of you, use this to your advantage.

- **The Classic:** Pop the question in a public park or while out for a quiet walk. Maybe at a fancy restaurant, where the waiter brings the ring for dessert. After all, it is hard to go wrong with her, a ring, and you down on bended knee. You can memorize a romantic poem, or make one up yourself. Or just simply tell her all the reasons you love her. No matter how many times you practice it in front of the mirror, you will be nervous. Remember, as long as you say something sweet and get out the words *Will you marry me*, you will be fine.

- **The Ball Game:** You see it often: the "Will you marry me?" splashed on the big screen at the football/baseball game. If this is a special place for the two of you, then go for it. If this is a special place for just you, then try another venue. There are women who love their teams just as much as you do, but it seems like there are so many other romantic options.

- **Third-Party Involvement:** If you are going to do something more complex, like surprise her at her office, or leave a trail of rose petals ending with you, a ring, and a proposal, then you may need to get friends or relatives involved in the scheme. You can always get restaurant personnel involved in the act—they will do just about anything you ask for a nice tip. Have them write it in chocolate drizzle on the dessert plate, or plan ahead with them to make a fortune cookie with that extra special fortune, "Will you marry me?"

No matter how you choose to proceed, the more creative and memorable you make your proposal for the two of you, the better.

For Your Fiancée

When it comes to your proposal, keep in mind that sometimes it's the little things that will make your BTB the happiest. In this particular case, the detail you should not overlook is getting down on one knee right before popping the question. It is symbolic and traditional, but also very romantic and scores you a lot of brownie points. It is a gesture that adds a note of class and tradition to the proceedings. It is also a symbolic way to bow as if receiving the honor of becoming her husband. So don't worry about getting your pants dirty; there is a dry cleaners close by. The cleaning bill is a fair tradeoff to add a little gentlemanly class to your proposal. ■

Mistakes to Avoid

We have covered some great ideas of what to include in your thoughts on proposing, but I would be remiss if I did not give you a few pointers on what *not* to do for your proposal. Let's take a quick minute to talk about some of the less desirable ideas when it comes to the proposal.

- **Loose Lips Sink Ships:** Come out of the blue. Be a man, make up your mind, and then take action. You don't need to spread the news to anyone beforehand. Some news is just too juicy for people to keep to themselves, and this is that kind of life-changing news. In today's world, a chatty friend can ruin the surprise in about fifteen seconds flat, assuming he has a decent cell signal.
- **Don't Involve Social Media:** Well, it should go without saying that you should not post a proposal on Facebook. It is something so personal and intimate; it is one of the few things that truly must be experienced together. Seeing her reaction will be one of those images you will never be able to (or want to) get out of your mind for the rest of your life.
- **Don't Lose the Ring:** It may seem obvious, but keep the ring somewhere safe and sound until it's time to pop the question. Have a safe spot where it lives, and don't feel neurotic if you find yourself checking on it frequently.

- **Don't Make It Too Complex:** Going to a nice restaurant with ambiance? Great idea. Having an overly convoluted plot involving a flash mob? Not so much. This is a thing of simplicity and beauty, and shouldn't need to be dressed up with flashy gimmicks. Keeping it simple will keep the focus where it should be and add a little elegance to the proceedings.

We could go on here, like how hiding the ring in your family goulash recipe may get you to the altar, but you may have to make a side trip to the emergency room first. So when making your plans, leave as little to chance as possible, add some personality and charm to it, and then steel your nerves and go for it! Good luck!

Will She Say Yes?

If you're lucky, you will know—because the possibility of marriage has already been discussed, or by hints that have been dropped—that you are on firm footing going into this proposal. However, you may also be going into it with some doubt in the air. Now, some guys do get totally shot down after a very public proposal, but if you think the time is right, and you two are in the right place in your relationship, then pull the trigger. Each relationship is different and only you—and your soon-to-be BTB—know when it's time.

Nuptial Knowledge

What is the "average" marriage age in the United States?

■ For first-timers, the average bride is twenty-seven years old, and the average groom is twenty-nine years old. ■

Get with the Wedding Program!

We are going to give you a "Get with the Wedding Program" section at the end of each chapter. But instead of recapping who the flower girl is, we are going to go ahead and recap some of the most important information from each chapter.

- You have found that special someone and decided to ask her to get married. Congratulations! That is the hardest part.
- Have you bought the ring yet? Remember, you will really be buying her two rings (and you will need one as well!). Create a budget and stick to it.
- When it comes to picking her engagement ring, remember that it's your job to know her and what kind of ring her heart desires. Is a diamond your girl's best friend? If it's not and she wants a pearl ring, it's up to you to know this.
- Put some thought into the proposal itself. It should be done in a manner that you—and your bride-to-be—are comfortable with. Whether you choose to make your proposal a public spectacle or pop the question when you're on bended knee during a quiet night at home is all up to you. Just don't lose that ring!

CHAPTER 2

Shout It from the Rooftops

Congratulations! Now that you and your beloved have decided to spend the rest of your lives together, it's time to tell the rest of the world. But how? Also, once that is done, the real work begins. You will need to start some preliminary wedding planning. But don't worry. Unlike the engagement ring, you can just ask your BTB what she wants this time.

Telling Family and Friends

When it comes to telling those closest to you, the personal touch is always nice. I know this next suggestion will not be the "cool" thing to do—as my daughters like to text me their questions and requests anytime we are more than four feet apart—but, although it's not trendy, pick up the phone and at least call your immediate family. Or better yet, have them over for dinner to make the announcement. No text or e-mail, please. Believe me, they will really appreciate it. Besides, there are still lots of folks like grandparents who don't really check their e-mail and would appreciate a good old-fashioned phone call—or even a visit! Imagine that . . .

But while you really should get on the ball and actually tell your close family members about your engagement either on the phone or in person, you probably don't have time to do this for everyone you know. If that sounds about right, here are some fun and modern ways for you to get the word out without calling everyone on your contacts list:

- **Post a Special Picture:** Maybe your Instagram followers would like to get a peek at the two of you toasting, or just your hands clasped together. Snapchat it, post it on Facebook, and Tweet it out to your peeps. Just know that all (or at least most) of those people will be thinking how much fun it will be to attend your wedding.

- **Send Out a Video:** If you're really into video or just like to play around with this kind of thing, you could make a really nice montage of classic wedding props spliced in with photos of you and your bride-to-be. It could even be the beginning of a nice wedding video. You can also use those skills you developed making the YouTube video of your dog fetching you a beer and put something together as an engagement announcement. Then it's just a matter of sending out the link.

- **Create a Wedding Website:** This one is now the norm instead of the exception. You can write up the proposal story for everyone to see, post photos, and do fun online polls on topics ranging from your wedding theme to whether or not blue should be the official color of your ceremony. This site can serve as a central spot for friends and family to see where you are registered, and you can also put up funny posts about your planning experience.

- **Throw an Engagement Party:** This idea isn't trendy, but think about throwing an engagement party. Let's review the basic concept: You are getting together the important people in your life to celebrate your engagement. See, it's not a totally crazy idea. Even if you just want to do it by having everyone over for dinner, it's more about the celebrating than the dollars spent.

- **Send Out Engagement Announcements or Save the Dates:** Soon you will begin your mass-marketing campaign for your wedding. This will include marketing support materials such as "save the date" reminders and mini-billboards, also known as announcements, alerting your closest friends and family about your event. Unfortunately you can't include anyone in these mailings (or e-mailings) that won't make the guest list for your wedding. But more on all that later.

Now, before you go ahead and tell your happy news to everyone in the world, keep in mind that mentioning your engagement on every social media site and in every blast e-mail could cause some to mistake receiving the announcement as some sort of tentative invite. Who knows which people you haven't spoken to in five years will take your Facebook post as a tentative invite? That said, once you guys have given this some discussion, and if you find yourselves in agreement that those who make assumptions are just going to have to handle the rejection, then go all out. While this may lead to many disappointed non-invitees, it really is their problem, not yours. And while you may be friends with people who are so excited about your wedding that they pretty much invite themselves to it, you may also find that some of your friends aren't as excited as you'd wish they would be . . .

Friends and Jealousy

If you and your bride-to-be are around the age where lots of your friends (or friends of your friends) are getting married, be prepared for some potentially odd reactions from, statistically speaking, at least one of those friends. There may be a couple out there who is teetering on the edge of their own proposal, but someone is holding out. So when you announce your engagement, your buddy may pull you aside and say something along the lines of, "Dude, you're making me look bad. I told my girl we were in no rush. Now all the pressure's on me!" Well, since you are neither his couple's counselor or therapist, he will need to take care of his own house. I thought I would warn you so you know why there is that friend of yours (or hers) who does not seem to be sharing in your joy.

For Your Fiancée

Sometimes your successes aren't met with the joy from your friends that you would expect. Getting engaged is one of those times, and it may happen to your BTB. Getting engaged by a certain time in their life is important to many, and if your fiancée jumps the line ahead of one of her friends, she may get a lukewarm reception to the announcement of the upcoming nuptials. This will be an easy test for you in the way of giving your BTB support when she needs it. A quick reminder of how it's disappointing that her friend reacted this way, but that it shouldn't affect the happiness the two of you are creating, should help. If the pep talk doesn't help, then just letting her vent and talk it through can be plan B. If neither of those works, just start asking questions about what she wants at the wedding to keep her focused on the positives in her life. ■

Choosing the Where and When

Okay, so you've told everyone you know that you're getting married. Now, once the initial excitement starts to wear off, you'll start to hear "So, have you set a date?" from every friend and family member eager to mark it down on the calendar. At this point, it's time to get serious about planning, so, just sit down with your fiancée and a bottle of wine and pick a time and place. Sounds easy, right? Well, unfortunately it is a little bit trickier than that. The first step is to decide where you want to hold your wedding. Then you can begin to make some sound decisions from that point on. Each time of year has its pluses and minuses, so let's break it down to see what works for you.

Choosing a Venue

The first thing you need to do is figure out where you want to hold your wedding reception and ceremony. Has your fiancée always dreamed about getting married on the beach? Do you really want to hold the reception in the hotel ballroom in your hometown so your elderly grandma can attend? These are all things that you have to figure out before you make any decisions on venue and date. If you have a dream venue in mind already, then its availability will drive the possible dates. Keep in mind that you and your bride-to-be won't always agree and the two of you will likely have to compromise to get something that you're both happy with. This can be tough, but doing this now lets you know what you're in for in the long haul. In Chapter 5, we talk more about how you can take a venue and make it your own, but as you're choosing your ceremony and reception venues, keep the following in mind:

For Your Fiancée

For some grooms, helping their BTB select a wedding venue boils down to one simple phrase: "Yes, dear." But it doesn't have to be that way. Imagine if you actually tried to add some value to the process! Yes, your duties may be nothing more than calling venues and scheduling site visits, but that is okay. Even if in the end your input doesn't amount to a whole lot more than a symbolic stamp of approval, it is better to stay, well, engaged in the process of planning the rest of your lives together. She will appreciate you getting in there and helping. ■

Size Matters

If you are going for a smaller, more intimate wedding where you only invite close friends and family, you will not need to reserve the conference center downtown. On the flip side, if you plan to invite everyone you've ever met (plus their plus-ones), then holding your ceremony in the backyard may not work, either. We discuss setting your guest list later on in this chapter, and it's something you'll really need to figure out before you book and pay out that retainer fee.

Visit First

One of my coworkers told me a story about her vacation the other day. She and her husband had decided to go away for a trip to celebrate their tenth wedding anniversary. They chose their hotel online and picked a local place that was a few dollars cheaper than the local big hotel chain. Upon arrival, she totally regretted her decision, as the pictures posted on the website were very deceptive. In short, the place was a dump. The point of my telling you this is not to encourage you to frequent big businesses but to encourage you to visit your wedding and reception venues in person before booking. There are just some things that you need to see with your own eyes. The only other lesson you could grab onto here is that not everything you see on the Internet is true, but I hope you already knew that.

Distance

You will need to keep in mind the distance your venue is from important areas. If you are doing a wedding near your hometown, but over an hour away, then you will need to have more hotel rooms blocked off for potential guests to stay overnight. If the venue is far away from the hotel, explore getting a shuttle service for guests to and from the various venues.

Weddings remind us that our lives have meaning and that love is the strongest bond, the happiest joy, and the loveliest healing we can ever experience.
—Daphne Rose Kingma, author and relationship expert

Timing Is Everything

Popular venues may be booked up to one or two years in advance. If you have your heart set on such a place, you may find yourself starring in your own personal version of *The Five-Year Engagement*. Evaluate the tradeoffs, such as how far off a venue is available and the cost of such a popular spot. There may be other alternatives available that are more suitable for your wedding size and time frame.

Even if you're interested in booking a less popular venue, those places tend to book up as well. Once you decide where you want to book, talk to the in-house wedding planner to help you figure out when the venue is actually available. If that's the spot you and your fiancée want and it's only available on the second Saturday in October, is that something you can live with? Your venue's availability may well set your date, so keep that in mind as you look.

Setting a Date

It's time to set the date for your wedding. Don't worry, you only have 365 choices! But realistically, most weddings take place on the weekend. Sit down with your fiancée and prioritize your selection criteria for your venue. Is the ability to hold a certain number of guests paramount to your "go big or go home" wedding philosophy? Or have the two of you decided that as long as your wedding is in your hometown you will be happy? Once these different factors fall into place in rank of importance, you will be getting somewhere. Let's investigate some of the traditional criteria couples consider.

Choose the Season

When it becomes time to think out your wedding date, you may wonder, "Where should we begin?" Well, instead of considering each and every day, you can start by looking at the seasons. Each season has its own feel, and you can play off that for your wedding. I mean, who wants to have a beach wedding in the winter?

- **Spring and Summer:** It is not much of a surprise that spring and summer weddings are the most popular. There is that warmth in the air, and flowers are blooming everywhere. In addition to nature working with you, many people are able to take vacations and the timing here can help make it easier for your valued attendees to make it to your soiree. Lastly—and a little selfishly—there are some killer honeymoon ideas to be had this time of year. And who doesn't want to spend a week on the beach or lounging about on a scenic cruise the week after you tie the knot?
- **Fall and Winter:** This can also be a spectacular time for the two of you to get hitched. If you dare to go outdoors, the fall foliage can provide a beautiful natural backdrop for your ceremony. Many couples have embraced the season by finding a snowy destination and using a ski lodge as their main venue. There are two issues with this time of year that you need to watch out for. If you are going to have Jack Frost on your guest list, be prepared for the possibility that a winter storm may affect your event, and may affect the ability of some of your guests to make it to your wedding. Also, if you allow your date to be set too far into the fall, it will bump up against the holiday

season and may cause a problem for guests who may end up having to choose between spending their travel budgets on you or their family. So when it comes to navigating the obstacle course that is picking a wedding date, what kind of conflicts do you need to look out for?

Nuptial Knowledge

What are the most popular months for weddings?

■ Browsing the various studies and data available, over a long term June is the most popular, followed by August and then September. Keep this in mind when planning. You'll need to book further in advance, and possibly pay more for the most in-demand venues and vendors during these times.

Outside Events

You do not have to worry about avoiding the weekend when the circus comes to town, but you should try to avoid overlapping your close relative's fortieth birthday weekend with your wedding. Your family may be understanding, but you don't want to run them over just so you can have it your way.

If you want to have a holiday wedding, Labor Day or another innocuous holiday that includes a built-in three-day weekend for your guests is often a nice way to go. If your guests are traveling, that will give them time to relax before the workweek starts up again. However, major holidays like Christmas can be problematic, as you are essentially asking guests to spend the holiday with you instead of with their families. I would avoid Thanksgiving and Christmas altogether. I feel like the rest of the holidays are fair game, as I have never heard of anyone having an extensive Labor Day celebration planned.

Vacation

Are you planning to take a nice honeymoon? Check with your and your fiancée's work schedules to make sure you are able to take time off for when you want to plan your trip. Plus, if you are paying your own way, you may need time to save up for it! If at all possible, try do something really special together. There will be only one chance to begin your lives together on a wonderful trip. Besides, America is filled with couples who are still trying to find the right time to take their first honeymoon five or ten years after their wedding.

A Special Date

Some couples like to be nostalgic and pick the anniversary of their first date or the date when they met. You can also look at parents' or grandparents' anniversary dates, in tribute to them. These kinds of choices are a nice way to add meaning to your date.

Setting the Guest List

Now that you are (hopefully) making progress on setting the date and location of your wedding, it's time to turn your attention to the next matter at hand: the guest list. Now before we really get into this, there's one thing that you need to keep in mind about your wedding: The day isn't about you. It's first about the bride, and then it more or less becomes a party for your family and friends. Don't worry though. You aren't getting cheated. After all, you're getting married to your dream girl, and you always have the wedding night and honeymoon to look forward to. But, anyway, about those guests . . . Who are they? Much like politics or the discussion you had with your fiancée about naming your new puppy, creating a guest list can be an emotional tug of war where it's every man for himself. But in love or war, there *are* a few rules that you need to keep in mind . . .

Keep It Even

Once you have picked the venue and considered the budget, you should know how many guests will be invited. (And if your guest list helped you decide on your venue, then this part is already taken care of! Good for you!) If possible, divide the number of guests that your venue can hold evenly between you, your future bride, and then her family/your family. If you can make this work, it's the best-case scenario for everyone, because it's, well, fair.

Keep It Quiet

If you remember, earlier in the chapter we mentioned that you should think about whether you want to tell everyone about your upcoming nuptials. If you made the decision to keep it quiet, hopefully your forethought has saved you from "long lost" friends (who clearly were lost for a reason) from e-mailing you saying their invitation must have gotten lost in the mail, but they can't wait to see you!

Stand Your Ground

Bullying is a serious issue, and in this case I am not talking about an old-fashioned playground beat down . . . although that may be a fair analogy. No, I am talking about one of the parents, usually one of the moms, trying to hog a disproportionate amount of invitations for her endless supply of friends/acquaintances. You have to stand your ground here, or you will end up only having a few people who are within ten years of your age group at your wedding. If you can't say no, at least your guest list—and your future mother-in-law—will be restrained by the size of the venue. If there is still room available, then sometimes you can decide—as a couple, I can't stress this enough!—to allow the offending parents to pay for their extra guests. Yes, I feel this should apply even if the offenders are the parents paying for the wedding.

For Your Fiancée

So what do you do if there is a "Momzilla" on the loose? Well, your role is not to get out of the way and watch the battle from a front row seat. If someone on your side of the family is causing the trouble, then you need to handle it. You may love your family, but you are going to be living with your wife. You need to intervene on her behalf. If it is her family, then a bit of diplomacy is required. Talk with your BTB and see if she wants to wrangle her family or if there is something you can do to help. If her solution is for you to confront her family on her behalf, then try to do so with a minimum of hurt feelings. Remember, you will potentially be spending lots of upcoming holidays with these folks. Hopefully, the problem is more a case of misunderstanding than anything else, and adults will act as such and clear up the issue. ■

Stay Up to Date

Are you inviting that long lost uncle who is remarried? Or did he get divorced again? Hey, didn't Auntie Rita just move to Dallas? I can't remember. Before you even get to the point where you're ready to send out invitations, make sure you have the right addresses and up-to-date information on your guests. More than one invitation has gone out with the wrong name of the current spouse on it or has gone to the wrong address, leaving Uncle Ernie wondering why he wasn't invited.

Nuptial Knowledge

How long is the average engagement period?

■ The average length of engagement is fourteen months according to a survey of 18,000 brides done by WeddingChannel. com. This is about thirteen months too long for most grooms.

Who to Cut?

Got too many people on the list? There is no telling which of these jokers you will stay in contact with five or ten years from now. When it comes to workplace friends/coworkers, it should usually be an all-or-nothing proposition. After all, are you really going to invite your peer but snub your boss? Do so at your own risk. What it basically boils down to is, which people do you really feel a connection with? Who do you want to try and cement a long-term friendship with? When it comes to old friends you haven't seen in ages or obscure cousins you barely know, just look at the list to see who you really want to make a part of your life. If your family is the priority, then the obscure cousin is in!

Kids or No Kids?

Many couples are choosing not to have children at their wedding celebration. The trick here is how to handle this decision gracefully. You will usually offend at least one parent who wants to bring her kids, so be ready for a little backlash. The next point for this situation is correctly wording the invitation. Don't say "No Kids Allowed" or especially "NO KIDS—PERIOD." You look bad, and besides, you have probably invited the grandparents, who are the "go-to" babysitters for many couples. So only print the names of the parents on the invitation, and get the word out among family and guests. Some people even set up childcare for their guests, although some parents will be hesitant to leave their kids with an unknown babysitter. Bottom line: It's your right not to have kids at your wedding, but don't expect everyone to agree with it.

A, B, and C?

The popular wisdom is to plan for a certain percentage of your invited guests to send their regrets and be unable to attend your wedding. You will see different theories depending on who you talk to, but most say that you can safely invite a few extra guests (10 percent of the total), counting on scheduling conflicts and the like to keep you at your desired total number of guests. These first recipients of the invitations are known as the "A-list" guests. You will then create a "B list," or people you want to invite if enough of the "A-listers" cannot make it, and so on.

Remember, you are taking your chances a little bit— if everyone decides to come, then you should be flattered, but also make sure your venue and budget can accommodate this scenario. In answer to your next question of how, I don't know. I guess the menu is now composed of: salad, chicken or steak, and unlimited chocolate fountain (first-come, first-served).

Get with the Wedding Program!

- When it comes to telling family and friends about your engagement, try to do something fun and personal. Inviting them all over for dinner to make the big announcement is always a hit.
- Technology can give you a great way to announce your wedding to the world. Use your social media skills to send out a fun picture and/or announcement.
- There are advantages and disadvantages to setting your wedding during the various times of the year. Consider the weather and likelihood of your guests being able to attend. June and August are the most popular months to be married, so if your heart is set on that time of year, it may require some extra planning, organization, and patience on your part.
- When it comes to planning around holidays, avoid the big ones like Thanksgiving and Christmas, where many families may have long-standing traditions that would make it difficult for them to attend. The holidays where people are generally off work but do not include major celebrations, like Labor Day, are better choices.
- Once you know your venue and date, begin to turn your attention to developing the guest list. Ideally you would split the number of invitations between yourself and your bride, with the respective families getting an equal amount of invitations to hand out. This should all be done within the framework of your overall budget.
- If there is a disagreement on how the invitations are being divided between families, you may have to step in

and mediate the problem. If your family members are causing the issue, you definitely must step in.

- Don't be surprised if there are some disagreements concerning who is invited and why your future in-laws can't have more invitations for their friends.

- You may need to set an "A" and "B" guest list, as not everyone you invite will be able to attend. As the "Regrets" come in, you can invite someone else. Just make sure to give them an appropriate amount of time before the wedding, so they don't feel like they were last on the list.

CHAPTER 3

Paying for the Wedding

So far, I have tried to give you as much concrete information as is available, but some of the topic matter lends itself more to opinion and conjecture. We are now getting to the heart of the matter, the budgeting and funding of the wedding. For some of you, those with generous family, you may be thinking to yourself, "I'm not paying, so what does it matter?" Believe me, it matters. Those who are paying for this celebration of your love, they have a budget, and they may give you some guidelines or limits that you need to consider when making your selections. For those of you who are paying for your own wedding, you already know this, and hopefully will pick up a few ideas from this section. So we'll examine a traditional list of costs, setting your budget, and if you are lucky, which family traditionally pays for which expense. So sharpen your pencil and ready your calculator; it's time to "figure out" your wedding budget.

What Are You Paying For?

Remember that WeddingChannel.com survey that I referenced earlier? You don't, do you? They looked at 18,000 weddings from 2011 and gave us some wedding data to digest. The average wedding cost was just north of $27,000! That's a lot of wedding cake! Don't freak out yet, unless you live in New York. That figure includes all of the Manhattan weddings, where the average wedding costs an overwhelming $65,000! Whew. It hurts my wallet just typing that. But with some prior planning and a little creativity, let's hope you can do better.

Now, are you prepared to be financially responsible, and make all the wise and prudent choices needed to walk the line between having your—and your fiancée's—dream wedding and falling off the "fiscal cliff"? Not everyone feels the need to throw a big wedding, and if you two crazy kids decide to run off to the justice of the peace, get married, and invite everyone to the corner pub, then more power to you. After all, if you look at your wedding as a purely financial transaction, you are basically throwing a huge party for your family and friends and, aside from some pretty cool gifts, you don't get a lot of concrete benefits out of the deal. But if you and your fiancée do want to go the "big party" route, then you need to know what you'll be paying for.

In the following sections, where we go over your possible expenses, you'll notice that we've included an estimated payment for each item as a guide; keep in mind these numbers may change depending on your location and on your personal preference. I know this section may have you considering a Betty Crocker wedding cake, but hang in there. That's why we are setting the budget now. And no matter how much you decide to spend, remember to make a budget and celebrate within your means; you'll find a worksheet at the end of the chapter that shows you how. There is no need to spend money you don't have and start off your lives together mired in debt. Focus on what's important to the two of you, prioritize, and enjoy your wedding!

Ceremony

When it comes to your wedding venue, the first decision you need to make is whether to hold the ceremony in a church or not. If you and your BTB are of different faiths and need help deciding how to handle that, well, please see Chapter 5. But if you want to hold your ceremony in a non-religious building, then just be creative. You can find some really cool and different venues such as a museum or an old turn-of-the-century home to hold it in. If you're looking to save on the venue expense, there is always the biggest house of a willing family member. Just know that churches usually ask for a donation, and wedding venues have a set fee depending on the time of year and number of guests.

If you do decide to hold the ceremony in a church, your costs will include the church and the decor. Don't sneeze at the mention of decor, as decking out the church and reception hall in fresh flowers can run up into the thousands if you decide to get fancy with it. There is also the cost of the Padre, even if he or she is an old family friend. Some ministers will simply ask for a donation to the parish they serve or to a worthy cause they support. Don't be the guy who whips out the $20 bill and makes the man of God feel like a jerk for telling you that you're low-balling him. You can always ask about average donation amounts or ask an assistant who works with your imam. The cost for the venue itself can vary due to the demand for the location and the time of year you are looking for. Many couples now are spending more on the entertainment and quality of the other reception items than on the venue itself. Oh, and I know I have made you out to have several different faiths, but I want everyone to feel at home. Shalom.

Average Cost: Wedding Officiate: $250; Wedding Venue: $500–$1,250

Reception

Your reception will (most likely) include food, music, decor, and the venue itself. Don't forget the entertainment, which is usually a live band or DJ playing from a list of music you suggest. I am not talking about Uncle Mike dusting off his clown suit and pulling an extra long hankie out of his jacket sleeve.

So what's the average cost? Sit down for this one. The average reception has about 150 people; you may have more or fewer guests based on the guest list we went over in the last chapter. Remember, you have to feed all of these folks, and if it's not against your personal oath or creed, give them all the opportunity to get drunk. This line item eats up about half of most people's budget. And the total is . . . drumroll please . . .

Average Cost: $10,000–$13,000 (Note: Throughout, just know that the standard tip, a.k.a. no one will call you a cheapskate behind your back, starts at 15 percent. If a provider does an outstanding job, you can tip more but are not required to do so.)

And if you don't book your DJ or band through your reception site, you'll be paying even more . . .

DJ or Band

The cost for DJ and band options varies widely. Looking at some options, I found several well-reviewed wedding bands ranging from $600–$5,000 for an event. Most of them will (and should) let you preview their music. If you choose a DJ, he should be well reviewed, and have liability insurance. Many DJs do a wedding package of four to five hours, with more time available upon request. Cost will vary, but many run something like $125 per hour. With either option, ask as many questions as possible.

- Does the entertainment provider require dinner/a meal?
- How frequently do they break?
- Are you paying for setup/breakdown time?

Just know what you are getting yourself into because they will set the tone for the reception/gathering.

Average Cost: As discussed, cost will vary. It seems you can pull this off for less, depending on who you book, but in general a DJ will run closer to an average of $900, while the average for a band will run closer to $3,000. You can tip the band 15 percent, or they may drink more than their share from the bar. It's your call on how much to tip, but mostly just see how the evening goes and if they are friendly, willing to work with your requests, and add to the overall event.

To keep your marriage brimming, With love in the wedding cup, Whenever you're wrong, admit it; Whenever you're right, shut up.

—Ogden Nash, poet

Wedding Cake

When we get to Chapter 8, we will talk about this subject in more detail, but just know that you'll need to "Let them eat cake!" But not too much . . . these suckers are more expensive than you'd think. Don't forget that you'll need a cake topper, cake serving set, and all the niceties.

Average Cost: The average wedding cake comes in around $500.

Flowers

You may have noticed that we discuss flowers as a wedding cost. If you've never bought flowers for your BTB, then shame on you. If you have, then you know that nice flowers can get expensive really fast. We will discuss this more in Chapter 8, but the average cost will often run at $1,500 or more. Don't forget, we're not just talking bouquets; we're doing centerpieces, reception decorations, boutonnieres, corsages, and even the petals for the flower girl to spread. It's (almost) enough to make you want to start a greenhouse of your own.

Average Cost: Like we discussed, there will be flowers everywhere. The average is around the $1,500 mark.

For Your Fiancée

You may not know the difference between a calla lily and a Stargazer lily, but trust me, your bride-to-be certainly does. So when she shows you pictures of flowers and asks what you like, be interested. It's likely that she already knows what she wants and just wants to include you in the decision. ■

Wedding Dress

It's just one dress, right? How much could it possibly cost? Well, I'm sorry to be the bearer of bad news, but the bride's wedding attire can be no small expense. The name of the person who designed the dress will add to the cost if it is someone of reputation. The materials and how much silk involved will also impact the sticker price. Then there is the craftsmanship, and how much work was required to be done by hand to create the dress. There are many factors that go into the dress and affect its price that some men don't appreciate. But if it makes you say "Wow!" when you see your BTB on the wedding day, that is worth a lot!

In addition, you might want to reserve some cash for her rehearsal dinner outfit as well. After all, that beautiful dress is reserved for the wedding only, guys.

Average Cost: While you can certainly find dresses both more (and less) expensive than the average, look to drop around $1,000.

Nuptial Knowledge

Why do brides wear white wedding dresses?

■ Legend has it that this tradition began in 1840 when Queen Victoria was married in a white dress. The tradition was set in stone when *Godey's Lady's Book*, published way back in 1849, stated, "Custom has decided, from the earliest ages, that white is the most fitting hue, whatever may be the material. It is an emblem of the purity and innocence of girlhood, and the unsullied heart she now yields to the chosen one." Women long ago stopped reading instruction manuals that told them how they should act, but for its symbolism the white dress hangs on.

Bridal Accessories and Styling

Yes, for you it may involve a razor, fingernail clippers, and a trip to the barbershop. But your BTB will want to be fussed over, and she will need more than a new razor. She will most likely need special hair and makeup, and many brides like to get a manicure and pedicure right before the big day. Let's not forget the dress doesn't come with shoes or a veil, so she will need these as well. Oh, how about earrings? Maybe they can be her something "borrowed"?

Average Cost: Veils alone are $150–$250. This line item will run at least $500 unless you are purchasing new diamond earrings. Then the budget for this will probably double.

Tux

We'll talk more about renting your tux in Chapter 7, but for now all you need to know is that some vendors will throw in your tux rental for free if all of your groomsmen rent their tuxes through their company. Not a bad deal—for you and your budget anyway. In addition, sometimes the groom's parents have been known to pick up the tux rental tab for the groom and his groomsmen.

Average Cost: $150

Stationery

Again, I understand that some of us will simply be utilizing the justice of the peace. But for those with the means and the desire, there will be some printing costs to undertake. Of course the invitations are pretty expensive. There is fancy (but nonfunctional) tissue paper often included in each envelope, and the "RSVP" materials, plus loads of postage. Don't forget, if you are going all out, you will be sending "Save the Date" cards and printing place cards for dinner seating and programs for the wedding. Save a tree (and a few bucks!) and send out some of these electronically! Hopefully some kind soul in your circle has presentably fancy handwriting; otherwise, you may get to add a calligrapher to your staff.

Average Cost: $250–$400

Favors

What exactly is a wedding favor? If you went to birthday parties growing up, and you received a gift bag with candy and toys in it when you left, then you get the general idea. If you are having "favors" for all the guests, you can see how this can get expensive in a hurry. You mean the guests are going to come to the wedding, eat and drink for free, enjoy the entertainment, and then you have to give them presents? Yep. That's why many in the past have cynically compared their reception to throwing a really nice party for their friends (and parents' friends!). Still confused? Favors may include customized wedding pens, coasters, playing cards, etc.

It is a thing now to give a donation to a charity in the guests' names in lieu of wedding favors. This is a nice gesture, as most wedding favors are small trinkets that do not impact the quality of the recipient's life to any great extent. If this option sounds good to you, discuss with your BTB and move forward. As a word of caution, pick a charity that is not politically oriented and that most reasonable minds can agree upon. This will minimize any potential drama for a guest who doesn't like your charity and wants to let your bride know this in the receiving line.

Average Cost: $250

Photography/Videography

We'll go over this in more detail in Chapter 8, but know that you can handle the photography/videography for your wedding in a number of different ways. You can of course hire a professional, who will stage the various shots of the wedding parties, families, and for sure the bride and groom. You can keep the photographer around to shoot the reception and take video messages from intoxicated or sentimental guests so you'll be able to enjoy a multimedia keepsake of your wedding day. You can also place disposable cameras on each table and let the untrained guests do the work for you. Or you can do both. Depending on your budget and how you slice it, there can be some flexibility on this item. Often the photographer will offer video services as well so you can have live-action keepsakes of your rowdy guests. This will add staff and cost to the bill, but it can be nice to have if the budget is there for it.

In addition, many couples hire the photographer to put together their wedding albums, which can add to the cost. If the album is something you want to do yourselves for cost or creativity reasons, make sure you own the rights to the pictures before you sign the contract.

Average Cost: These seem to really have a wide range, but I am hearing about $1,500–$2,000 for a true professional. If you are really unsure, take a test drive: Book them to do an engagement photo session and see what happens results-wise. You will know if you can work with them on the big event after that. Should you tip these people? That's a personal preference. If they are putting up with a lot of special requests and drunken guests, then maybe they earned it as a sort of battle pay. The standard is fine, but I bet if you slip the photographer a few extra $20s, he will be just fine with that.

Transportation

We'll talk more about transportation in Chapter 8, but for now, you are throwing this wonderful wedding bash. It would be nice to arrive in style, right? Some couples like to take a private ride to reflect with each other on the ride from the church to the reception. Others like to load their respective wedding parties into a limo and have a glass of champagne. This is of course not a mandatory expense, especially if you have your own car. But it's a nice touch if you have the right kind of budget, and this is really one of the times you do not want to be driving yourself around. After the ceremony, having you and your new bride together in the car can really help you enjoy your first moments together as a newly wedded couple. Reflect on the meaning of the ceremony, talk about your favorite parts of the ceremony, or just toss back that champagne and breathe a sigh of relief that you made it through the first part of the day. Well, these are the nice and honorable ideas for correct use of the limo ride.

Average Cost: $600–$750. Before you tip, make sure the tip wasn't already included by the limo company. Otherwise, our standard 15 percent rate applies.

The Wedding Planner

Okay, I wasn't going to include this one, if simply because it made me feel slightly pretentious. In today's economy, with so many people working so hard to make ends meet, it just seemed like it wasn't applicable. However, it seems that about one in three couples are now hiring wedding planners, mostly to handle the events on the actual day of the wedding. This is as opposed to the Jennifer Lopez kind that handles every detail, from start to finish, including stealing the groom (just kidding).

Average Cost: For day of the wedding planner: $1,200–$1,500; For total event planner: $3,500–$4,000 (keep in mind that wedding planners' fees can run all the way north of $10,000). I have never used a wedding planner, but I feel like they are professionals and not service providers. Just go ahead and pay their invoice.

Rehearsal Dinner

This is the dinner that follows a rehearsal of the wedding ceremony and is usually held the night before the wedding. You'll want to invite your and your bride-to-be's (immediate) families, the wedding party and their spouses if they have them, as well as the priest/minister/rabbi/etc. and his or her spouse, if the situation is such that they have one. The next slice into the budget would be to invite all of your out-of-town family who traveled to attend the wedding. Then, if your budget will hold it, you can add *all* of your out-of-town guests, if you like. You'll find more info on the rehearsal dinner in Chapter 9, but this can be a pretty expensive night. This line item includes food, invitations, entertainment (if any), and decor (if any). You can imagine the wide range of cost possibilities here, depending on the size of your budget.

Average Cost: $1,000

Rings

We've already talked about the engagement ring, but you still need to think about getting your bride her wedding band. The trend here leans toward bands made of white gold or platinum. A recent study (that pesky WeddingChannel.com survey) shows about 65 percent of brides are "somewhat" involved in picking their wedding bands. If you're curious where I stand on this matter, pick it out yourself. In addition, you'll need your own wedding band. The groom's ring often matches the bride's in terms of the metal used and overall style. This is setting you up for a lifetime of your ties, sweaters, and various other clothing items being predetermined by the choices of your spouse. Have fun!

Average Cost: $6,000 + $350–$450 for your wedding band. A little insight into my math here: I am putting you down for $5,000 for the engagement ring alone, another $1,000 for the wedding band for her, and then an additional $350–$450 for your ring. Yes, you can find very nice ring sets for less money, and I found many very nice ones in just a few minutes of searching the web. But many studies show the average engagement ring is somewhere around $5,000. So I just want to let you know what's going on out there, and you can adjust accordingly.

Marriage License

A quick crash course on marriage license procedure: Around a month before your wedding date, use a little detective work to find out where you need to go to obtain your wedding license for the state you are getting married in. Many states are similar, but also have a few differences. For example, in New York, you begin the form online and then go to the city clerk together. You cannot appear separately and no one may show up on your behalf. You complete the form in the office, show proof of divorce if previously married, and present a proper form of ID from the list shown online. Then the celebrant who performs the ceremony must return the form after the ceremony. Read your state-specific information to see if there are any other requirements. If you don't get a marriage license, you guys are just playing dress-up . . . at least in the eyes of your elected officials.

Average Cost: $50

Gifts

It is tradition for the bride and groom to buy gifts for their wedding party. For those brave souls who gave speeches like the best man, or wore melon-colored frocks like the bridal party, you figure they've probably earned a little something. For the groomsmen, I feel like flasks are always on the list. Let's change it up and consider getting all the groomsmen tickets to a sporting event or concert they can attend together. Your BTB is responsible for the bridesmaid gifts, but if she asks, be ready with a quick wine of the month club or massage gift certificate suggestion.

Average Cost: I will put you down for at least $50 per groomsmen, and a cool $100 for the best man.

So there you have it, the cost estimates and breakdown of the main expenses. It's a pretty daunting list, I will admit.

To love someone deeply gives you strength.
Being loved by someone deeply gives you courage.
—Lao Tzu, philosopher

Who's Paying for What

Many wedding traditions are linked back to the times when the bride's family paid the groom's family a dowry, a payment of money, goods, or land. This outdated custom may still be alive in some parts of the world, but not here in the old U-S-of-A. Somehow this got twisted into a custom where the bride's family coughed up large sums of money to pay for many major wedding expenses. If you have family that is willing and able to make a major contribution to your wedding, then consider yourself lucky. Is it appropriate for you to ask your parents for financial help for your wedding? I cannot answer that because I do not know you or your parents. But you can probably gauge the type of relationship you have with them and come up with an answer. If you are not sure if your parents (or her parents) are helping with any part of the wedding, the best thing to do is simply ask, but if you have an established career and your retired parents are living on a fixed income, then just make your plans and let them come to you. After all, they already gave you the gift of life, and probably played a major role in getting you to this point. What more do you expect from them?

For those in the circumstance where your families are going to be making a major contribution, then there are traditions that are usually followed. I know these things are changing rapidly, but I still feel there will be some of you who will be going down this path. In the following table, you'll see the traditional breakdown of who pays for what. Oh, and don't forget that the dowry of ten sheep goes to the bride's family.

Traditional Expenses or Who Pays for What	
Groom and Groom's Family	**Bride and Bride's Family**
Marriage license/Officiant's fee	Ceremony venue and music
Bride's engagement ring and wedding band	Groom's wedding band
Bride's bouquet, grooms-men's boutonnieres	Bridesmaids' bouquets and flowers for ceremony and reception
Rehearsal dinner	Reception costs (including music, food, decorations, etc.)
Tuxes for groom and groomsmen	Wedding gown and accessories
Honeymoon	Photography/Videography
	Stationery (including save the dates, invitations, programs, seating cards, etc.)
	Transportation

Although it might be great if your families want to pay for your wedding, again, don't expect anything. Those funds are often needed for more practical expenses. Also, the more you and your bride-to-be pay for on your own, the more control over the proceedings and various guest lists you will have. You will also have more control over any potential drama, since you will be having the final say in most matters. The more your or her parents begin to shell out the large amount of cash required for most weddings, the greater the potential for them to want to address some of the details they may want to include or certain guests they want to add. If you are in a very positive relationship with your parents and future in-laws, then my warnings may all be for naught. But all you have to do is talk to a few friends or spend a few minutes with a wedding planner, and the stories of Shakespearean-level drama will be easy to find.

Nuptial Knowledge

What percentage of couples pay some portion of their wedding expenses?

■ According to multiple wedding-related studies, about 75 percent. Less and less common are the days when the families cough up their retirement savings for a good party.

Setting a Budget

So, we have done a lot of nice talking about budgets, but what is this thing really going to cost? It's time to put something down and stick to it. Take the amount that you and your BTB have saved, plus any amount you can add to the pot over the engagement period before final payments may be due. Add amounts that generous family members or parents are adding. If your parents simply say, "We've got the rehearsal dinner covered," great, then simply allot a $0 for that. Then talk to them and see what they have in mind for that event. So without further ado, it's time to start your budgeting!

Wedding Budget Worksheet

Item	Projected Cost (including tax, if applicable)	Deposit Paid	Balance Due	Who Pays?
Wedding Consultant				
Fee				
Tip (usually 15–20%)				
Rehearsal Dinner				
Site rental				
Equipment rental				
Invitations				
Food and beverages				
Decorations				
Party favors				
Ceremony				
Location fee				
Officiant's fee				
Donation to church				

Item	Projected Cost (including tax, if applicable)	Deposit Paid	Balance Due	Who Pays?
On-site musician				
Tip for on-site musician				
Other musicians				
Tip for other musicians				
Program				
Aisle runner				
Business and Legal Matters				
Marriage license				
Wedding Jewelry				
Engagement ring				
Bride's wedding band				
Groom's wedding band				
Bride's Formalwear				
Wedding dress				
Alterations				

Item	Projected Cost (including tax, if applicable)	Deposit Paid	Balance Due	Who Pays?
Undergarments (slip, bustier, hosiery, etc.)				
Veil or headpiece				
Shoes				
Jewelry (excluding engagement ring and wedding band)				
Cosmetics or makeup stylist				
Hair stylist				
Groom's Formalwear				
Tux				
Shoes				
Gifts				
Bridesmaids				
Groomsmen				

Item	Projected Cost (including tax, if applicable)	Deposit Paid	Balance Due	Who Pays?
Reception				
Site rental				
Equipment rental (chairs, chair covers, tents, etc.)				
Decorations				
Servers, bartenders				
Hors d'oeuvres				
Entrées				
Meals for hired help				
Bar tab				
Toasting glasses				
Guest book				
Place cards				
Wedding favors				

Item	Projected Cost (including tax, if applicable)	Deposit Paid	Balance Due	Who Pays?
Tip for caterer or banquet manager (usually 15–20% total)				
Tip for servers, bartenders (usually 15–20% total)				
Photography and Videography				
Photographer's fee				
Wedding prints				
Album				
Parents' albums				
Extra prints				
Videographer's fee				
Video/DVD				
Reception Music				
Musicians for cocktail hour				

Item	Projected Cost (including tax, if applicable)	Deposit Paid	Balance Due	Who Pays?
Tip (optional, up to 15%)				
Live band				
Tip (optional, usually $25 per band member)				
Disc jockey				
Tip (optional, usually 15–20%)				
Flowers				
Flowers for wedding site				
Bride's bouquet				
Bridesmaids' flowers				
Boutonnieres				
Corsages				
Flowers for reception site				
Table centerpieces				
Head table				

Item	Projected Cost (including tax, if applicable)	Deposit Paid	Balance Due	Who Pays?
Cake table				
Wedding Invitations and Stationery				
Save the dates				
Invitations				
Thank-you notes				
Calligrapher				
Postage				
Wedding Cake				
Wedding cake				
Groom's cake				
Cake top and decorations				
Cake serving set				
Wedding Transportation				
Limousines or rented cars				
Guest transportation (if needed)				

Item	Projected Cost (including tax, if applicable)	Deposit Paid	Balance Due	Who Pays?
Tip for drivers (usually 15–20%)				
Honeymoon				
Transportation				
Accommodations				
Meals				
Spending money				
Additional Expenses (list below)				
Total of All Expenses				

Get with the Wedding Program!

- Before you set any plans in stone, you will need to make a wedding budget. Just like budgets come in all sizes, there is a wedding to fit every budget!
- The reception is a huge expense, usually soaking up close to 50 percent of a couple's wedding budget. This is due to the fact that you are feeding all the guests, and oftentimes providing adult beverages for them as well.
- If your parents can/will help, that's great. But the number of weddings fully parent-funded is on the decline. If you pay for your own wedding, it will give you more control of the proceedings and less drama.
- First you see how much is in your budget; then you prioritize the costs that you want to spend the money on. It sounds simple until you get out there and start looking at venues, dresses, caterers, etc. You will want the best of the best of everything!
- Remember, in the end it will not be important in ten years if your guests were served a gourmet meal, or if your rehearsal dinner was held at a trendy restaurant. These details will fade over time. What will last is the love the two of you have for each other and your lives together.

CHAPTER 4

Keeping with— and Breaking from—Tradition

Weddings are events steeped in tradition. From the white dress to throwing rice to the penguin-like appearance of the groom, you can probably picture some of the classic traditions in your mind. Many of these time-honored traditions are nice, and the meaning, sentiment, and symbolism behind them can only add to your ceremony. Also, depending on your particular faith, many of the customs you choose to follow can be tied up in your religion. Mazel tov! One of the final advantages of following traditions is that many of the major decisions are taken off your hands, and you can feel confident knowing you are doing things by an age-old tradition, which in some ways makes it feel "right."

However, as much as traditions play a role in the world of weddings, you should always remember that it's your party, so cry if you want to, meaning that this is your and your future wife's show and you shouldn't be afraid to do things the way the two of you want to do them. Keep some traditions, but do not be afraid to add to them and make your own. The two of you should discuss what traditions are important to one or both of you—and which ones aren't—and then present a united front to the rest of the world. So while you may end up fighting with your friends or relatives, or her friends and relatives, just make sure the two of you don't end up in an argument. There will be plenty of time for that after the ceremony . . .

For Your Fiancée

Your wedding is going to be a quick litmus test of things to come for your lives together. It has all of the hallmarks of your lives together going forward: potential money disagreements, meddling friends and family, and potential disagreements at every turn. The thing to keep in mind, to hold closest to your heart, is that you love this woman, and you will not let anything get in the way of that. Be involved in the planning of the wedding, but remember, even if you lose on every wedding-related issue that you disagree about, in the end you still win! So do not let wedding issues blow themselves up into anything bigger than what they really are. Hopefully you and your BTB can be the rock in the center of all of the wedding madness going on around you. ■

Who Does What

What we will do in this chapter is take a look at what each person's role is during a traditional wedding. Traditions are important to give meaning and depth to the proceedings. You and your BTB will be taking part in a ceremony that has been done hundreds of thousands of times. These traditional roles are dynamic, meaning if there are changes to be made in the overall framework that fit your wedding better, then that is great. Let's explore these roles and what general part they play in the wedding.

Bride

What are your bride-to-be's duties? Well, traditionally she has so many duties, it's hard to cram them all into this chapter. She is the filter through which just about every decision flows. She is in charge of the wedding, with responsibilities ranging from getting herself beautiful (or even more beautiful than she already is), to making sure the church ceremony and reception go off without a hitch, to making sure everyone just loves every inch of the wedding, which is what most brides hope will happen. At the same time, she is to be classically ravishing in her dress, not let anyone see her stress, and give a strong "I do!" when the time calls for it. She is responsible for cakes, flowers, multimedia documentation, entertaining the guests, having quality entertainment, and for making sure the minibars in the out-of-town guests' hotel rooms are stocked properly. By mentioning all this, I hope to paint a picture of how it is so easy for a bride to become overwhelmed. She can feel the extreme pressure that comes with knowing that all eyes will be on her, and striving for perfection on her big day. It's a lot for her to handle and it gives you one of your most important responsibilities of the entire wedding planning process: Don't let your loving, amazing bride-to-be become a bridezilla.

What's a Bridezilla?

The term references an out-of-control bride who has lost perspective . . . or, at the very least, her mind. When you ask many grooms how they know when their fiancées are turning into bridezillas, you'll commonly hear something like,

"I know it when I see it." But just in case you need some info on what to look for, here are a few clues that can help:

- **Grrrrr!**: Hear the roar of the bridezilla, like a T-rex on the hunt. She becomes irritable and angry upon any signs of resistance to her demands. It doesn't matter who is the voice of dissent; it could be her maid of honor, her mother, even you for that matter. Your bridezilla will feel that any resistance must be crushed, and disloyalty to the wedding tiara will not be tolerated.

- **Disregard for the budget:** Whether your budget is large or small, you need to stay within it. If your bride-to-be has transformed on you, you may hear justifications for extra costs, such as "Well, it's the best" or "I had to pick that one, everything must be perfect!" This is most likely not a sign that your future bride is greedy or irresponsible, but more that she is feeling overwhelmed. It may be time for you to become more engaged, help her delegate more of the wedding preparations, and let her know that everyone is there to support the two of you, not to tear you down. Well, most of them anyway. But the rest can poke themselves in the eye with a shrimp fork.

- **All-consuming passion:** You notice that your bride-to-be is talking to you day and night about wedding details. As you are kissing her neck, tempting your pre-wedding celibacy vow, she is mumbling about lilies. You overhear her on a call to her manager discussing the possibility of having the next few Fridays off so she can catch up on the wedding stuff.

- **Hostage demands:** If you find that your once sweet and loving fiancée is starting to issue signed executive orders for you and the maid of honor to carry out, then you may have a problem. For example, if you begin receiving directives like "Brian was short with me on the phone last week, he is uninvited" and "Make sure all the attendees know not to wear lavender, it's reserved for my bridesmaids," your bride has likely gone drunk with power, and you need to lead an intervention effort.

Some of these are in jest, but heavy is the head that wears the tiara. Many brides go from relishing the opportunity to plan their wedding to being stressed out and worried that the whole thing will be a train wreck. That pressure can cause them to be stressed out and unreasonable.

How to Help

When the stress kicks in, it is important that you be there for her. See what help you and others can provide to take some of the work off your BTB's plate. Rally her family and the maid of honor to make sure the bride knows she has a lot of help and that this huge project is something she doesn't have to plan all by herself. Take a planning task, complete it yourself, and when she meets you at the appointed time, just go out to dinner instead. Excitement and anticipation about the event are great; stress and worry are less great. Make sure she knows that you haven't checked out and, like many things over the rest of your lifetimes, you will be doing this together.

Okay, so now let's turn our attention to *you*.

Groom

Hmmmm, let's see. The wedding is at 4 P.M. So you need to get up around noon, shave and shower, slip into your monkey suit, get to the church a few hours early, and tell old war stories and cut up with your groomsmen. Does that about cover it?

Sorry guys, that to-do list is outdated by about thirty years. First and foremost, you need to find ways to get involved in the wedding planning phase without interfering with the things the bride is actually looking forward to. She *wants* to quibble over certain varying types of frosting and designs for the wedding cake. She cares about the flowers, and she of course wants to listen to all of those wedding band samples and look at every photographer's sample work. Now, you can be involved in these matters as much as you want, and in fact, you'll probably be required to be involved in them to some minimal degree even if you are saying to yourself, "Self, I have no interest at all in these matters." Too bad. You'll have to at least feign an interest for your bride. Trust me, she'll appreciate it!

So what can you do? Well, if one doesn't already exist, you can construct a database of all the (potential) guests and their details. You can get with your parents and your future in-laws to get the proposed guest additions. You can be the keeper of the budget, making sure the whole event stays on track financially. Organize the trip for both of you to head down and get your marriage license. All of these things are great to put on your list because they are not things that are really fun, but they are not things that you can really mess up, either. This will help your bride-to-be manage her stress levels (notice I didn't say eliminate) and free her up to focus on the things she would rather be doing.

Also, there is a list of things you can*not* do (seriously, don't even think about doing them; it will end badly) to make the wedding go smoothly.

- Don't go tooth and nail with her so you and your groomsmen can wear a throwback powder blue tux with ruffled shirt.
- Don't insist on having your friend that she doesn't really care for as one of your groomsmen.
- Don't put it all on her; you're getting married, too.
- Don't shrug at every little decision about flowers or place cards. I know you may not really care. But you do really care about your BTB and your lives together, so reach deep down and get some enthusiasm! If you continue to respond to everything with a sarcastic comment or shrug of the shoulders, it will seem like you are thinking the entire thing is beneath you. So let's not go there!

This is just a partial list of things you can do (or not do, as the case may be) to help the process run smoothly for both of you. Besides, you want your lives together to get off to a smashing start, and you definitely *don't* want to start off the honeymoon in a disagreeable mood because the wedding plans blew up on you, right?

Best Man

The "best man"? Really, in this wedding where the bride is queen, shouldn't you, the groom, bear this title? Just kidding. Traditionally, the best man is *your* best man, a tried-and-true friend who will hopefully be up to the task of being a positive impact on the festivities, give a killer speech, and

keep any embarrassing secrets you have in the vault—where
they belong.

We'll talk about your best man's role in more detail in
Chapter 6, but he really does have a lot to do, including:

- **Visit the Venue:** In my wedding experiences, people
  reflexively ask persons in the wedding party where
  restrooms are, the best way to get to the reception
  from the church, etc. Arm your best man with this
  info so these people don't bother you.
- **Plan the Bachelor Party:** For the bachelor party, the
  best man has the responsibility to plan activities that
  are fun, memorable, and will not under any circumstances end the evening with anyone going to jail.
  While you can give suggestions of things you want to
  do, and guidelines on how much alcohol you would
  like to be involved, it is the best man's job to roll with
  your guidelines and respect your request. If you have
  some doubts about whether he can pull this off, don't
  be afraid to mandate that your dad, uncles, etc., be
  involved because family is important to you.
- **Calm You Down:** The best man is also traditionally
  responsible for calming the groom's nerves (if any), a
  duty best summed up by the catchall phrase "getting
  the groom to the church on time." This also includes
  any case of cold feet or last-second doubt, where the
  best man is to give you, the groom, a not-so-gentle
  push in the right direction (toward the church).
- **Carry the Bride's Ring:** In addition to the bachelor
  party, the best man usually carries the bride's ring.
  This is one more reason to select a best man who fits
  the job title. Nothing would be worse than to come

to that part of the ceremony, only to discover the ring is missing. In my first turn as best man, I was clutching the ring as if my life depended on it.

- **Give a Speech:** The best man's speech is a time-honored tradition with murky beginnings. Best I can tell, it was a chance for someone to get up and vouch for the groom's character and intentions. In today's world, it is a great way to have your buddy give you and the bride a nice introduction and welcome into the world of marital bliss. While he needs to write it, do not be shy about working with your best man on his speech. He will in a way represent you to all of your family and friends. He should welcome the guests, thank the parents, and tell a few very mild stories. Then he can bless the happy couple, maybe work in a famous quote, and get out of there.

- **Tip Your Vendors:** If you want to make a clean getaway (and you will), you can give the best man all kinds of fun tasks to take care of for you. That is just another reason to pick a friend with a little bit of responsibility in his makeup. Included in these tasks will be the chance for you to give him envelopes with tips labeled for each service provider. He can hand these out at the end of the night after you and your bride have taken off in the limo.

- **Help Your Guests Home:** Lastly, since you and your new bride will be leaving to begin your new lives together, it doesn't hurt to ask the best man to round up a few helpers and get everyone safely back to their hotel or wherever they are resting their heads that night. You can arrange a shuttle back to the wedding hotel, or give him a few bucks to help encourage people to take cabs, etc., if it looks like there was a lot of participation at the bar that evening.

No wonder you have to buy the wedding party gifts! But that is why it's important to pick great friends or family for these roles, because they are helping you celebrate and doing some work for you also. Let's see what the maid of honor needs to be responsible for.

Maid of Honor

Oh, the maid of honor. Keep an eye on who gets selected to this position, because you will be seeing a lot of her during the engagement. Basically this woman (with all due respect to Patrick Dempsey's "Tom") is expected to clear out as much time as the bride needs for wedding planning activities. She may be asked to visit potential wedding locations, shop for wedding dresses, sift through the cake selection process, and host the bridal shower and bachelorette party. Other responsibilities may include reeling the bride in when she is out of control, and keeping the bride from losing her mind when she is having a bad day and suddenly wants to wear a black wedding gown. Whoever fills this role deserves a gift (and often gets one) because she is taking some of the heat off you and being a sounding board for the bride and all of her ideas.

And that doesn't even really cover the many duties that the maid of honor will be responsible for on the wedding day. She will most likely serve as a messenger service between the bride and groom, hold on to your ring, and will usually give a toast somewhere along the way. If that sounds like a lot of responsibility, remember, they don't call her a *maid* of honor for nothing.

Father of the Bride

The father of the bride has some really important scenes in this production as well. One of the most cherished is walking the bride down the aisle, to symbolically give his daughter away to the groom. It's Dad's last chance to call her his little girl, and spend a private minute beforehand with her.

The father-daughter dance is another touching moment. At the reception there will often be a moment when they clear the dance floor for dear old Dad to get a dance with his daughter. It's another moment recognizing the daughter moving forward in her life and becoming more independent.

The last duties for the father of the bride are a little different in their nature. One that may or may not be feasible is the hope of every young couple that the bride's father will make a sizable contribution to the wedding fund. Lastly, many look to the father of the bride to keep an eye on his wife, the mother of the bride, and reign her in as needed.

Mother of the Bride

We try to shoot straight with our readers on most topics, and the role and reality of the mother of the bride will be no exception. The simple truth is that the majority of moms are wonderful people who perfectly play their intended role in the proceedings. They are accommodating and supportive, and they generally are a great resource to help the event come off as smoothly as possible. Then there are a few who are probably truly wonderful people, but they seem to have forgotten this at their daughter's wedding. They become true "Momzillas," if you will, commenting on bridesmaids' appearances in a negative way, or asking her other daughters when they will finally get married. They may feel the need to belittle guests as well. They try to take over the planning, or dictate lists of guests that simply must be invited, even if you and your BTB have no idea who they are. No source of drama and controversy seems beyond their reach. The best way to manage these moms who choose to be disruptive forces to the wedding is to work with them where possible. Keep her involved in some part of the wedding planning and give her special projects to do. She did give birth to your BTB after all.

Happy marriages begin when we marry the ones we love,

and they blossom when we love the ones we marry.

—Tom Mullen, author

Father of the Groom

At first glance, it may seem like the father of the groom's duties and responsibilities are mostly limited to the wallet-related kind. He traditionally pays for the rehearsal dinner and a few other odds and ends if he can. In today's "everything goes" world, he may end up paying for more than that if he can. But the father of the groom also has several less structured, but very important duties to attend to:

- **Backup Best Man:** Let's face it, the father of the groom has a lot more life experience than the best man probably does. So the father of the groom can be on alert for the best man making "poor choices" about the bachelor party, etc., and be around if the groom needs some timely advice due to unscheduled nerves, cold feet, and the like.

- **Family Matters:** The groom is busy during a lot of the ceremony (of course) and throughout the reception. One item the FOG (father of the groom) can handle is wrangling unruly family members and guests on his side of the aisle. Is his recently divorced friend, fifty-year-old Nick, spending a little too much time with the bridesmaids? He can steer him away from the under-thirty crowd and focus his attention elsewhere. Maybe some relatives didn't get the memo, or need lots of hand holding. The FOG can be there for them.

- **Bring Your Dancin' Shoes:** The FOG will often lead his dance partner onto the floor shortly after the first dance has begun. Check with your bride-to-be to see how she'd like to play it.

- **Speech:** The FOG doesn't traditionally have a speech to give, although he may give a small one at the rehearsal dinner. In today's etiquette, if the groom's parents are paying for half of everything wedding-related, or the bride's and groom's parents are paying equal shares of the costs, the FOG and the father of the bride may both give speeches, since financially they are cohosts of the big event.

So the FOG only has small "official" duties, but he plays an important role. He has to be versatile and ready with a kind or supportive word, a quick speech, or a few words of wisdom for a frightened groom. This man has worked hard and has given a lot for you along the way, so make sure you find a quiet moment just to say "Thanks, Dad."

Mother of the Groom

The months surrounding the wedding might be a tough time for your mom since the event swirls around and focuses on the new lady in your life. So don't let her be the forgotten one during all of this wedding madness. Help your fiancée keep your mother involved to some degree. Get some e-mails going to ask her opinion on different wedding issues. And do what you can to let her know she is still an important part of your—and your bride-to-be's—life going forward. You want your mom and your soon-to-be wife to have a positive relationship if at all possible.

When Do They Do It?

The easiest way to make sure that everyone shows up when and where they are supposed to is to have it all planned out beforehand. Give each person clear and concise instructions on his or her role. For the best man (and maid of honor), you and your fiancée may want to take them to lunch and let them know what is in store for them if they have never been in this role before. For the rest, you may want to call them and let them know what you need them to do. Be specific so they know what you are asking them to do.

It may just be easiest to create an "All Things Wedding" website for the event. You can list each part of the wedding (rehearsal dinner, ceremony, reception) complete with addresses, contact information, a list of who should be there and when, as well as directions. Between laptops, tablets, and smartphones, there doesn't seem to be any way that anyone in your bridal party could be late! Having an electronic schedule will also allow you to easily make changes and communicate them to all parties. This is a huge improvement from the days long ago when any and all changes were met by a series of phone calls.

Nuptial Knowledge

What does each item in the old phrase "something old, something new, something borrowed, something blue" symbolize?

■ Each phrase represents something different and important in its own right. The something "old" represents good luck passed on from the previous owner, usually a family member. Something "new" is symbolic of a blessed future ahead of you. Something "borrowed" is to represent the well wishes of the owner of the item. The something "blue," the least intuitive of them all, is to represent loyalty and a stable, prosperous life. The rhyme used to include the phrase "and a brand new penny in my shoe." for good luck. I guess somewhere along the way brides didn't like using their shoes as a change purse and got rid of this part of the saying.

Decide Which Traditions Work for You(r Fiancée)

When it comes to what traditions you and your fiancée are going to follow, the two of you need to have a discussion to make sure you are both on the same page. This is especially true if you are of different religious backgrounds or have extremely strong traditions relating back to your heritage. If you can tackle these differences, it will get your marriage off to a great start by proving you can work through disagreements. On the case of religious differences between the two families, these differences are difficult to resolve. It can be done, so be creative and try not to hurt each other's feelings. Couples have even received a double blessing, one from a celebrant of each religion. If there is a simpler tradition, then make the old tradition new by putting your own spin on it. Brainstorm ideas together until you find a solution that suits you both. If all else fails, double-check what you are fighting about, and see if it is something that you will care about in twelve months. If it doesn't pass that test, you are probably okay just to let it go and let your BTB notch the victory. It is a matter of knowing the difference between what's important to you and what is important because you really like to win when you are in an argument. Try to know yourself and know the difference.

I used to think a wedding was a simple affair.

Boy and girl meet, they fall in love, he buys a ring, she buys a dress, they say I do. I was wrong. That's getting married.

A wedding is an entirely different proposition.

—Steve Martin as George Banks in Father of the Bride

Old Traditions, New Trends

Many of the wedding traditions are steeped in cultures long gone from today's world, and many can be swept aside without a second thought if you and your bride-to-be so choose. There is nothing wrong with keeping the heart of the tradition, yet putting a unique spin on it. And, in today's brave new world, many couples have been doing just that in order to make sure their weddings are personal and fit into their pictures of the big day. For the most part, these trailblazers are keeping the basic structure of the wedding itself (nearly 70 percent of all weddings still take place in a church), but for all of the tradition that is a part of many weddings, there are also trends that sweep through like a one-hit wonder. I am not talking about whether or not the color yellow is trendy or whether the "chevron" pattern is hot. I am talking about new ideas in the wedding world that seem like they will be around for a while. It will be up to you and your fiancée whether you want to incorporate these into your own ceremony. Let's take a look at a few of the burning trends right now:

Pinterest Weddings

I am not going to be as lame as to explain the concept behind Pinterest to you. You (or at least your bride-to-be) are probably already way ahead of the curve on this. But the beauty of Pinterest is that you no longer have to rely on your own creativity to make your wedding experience unique, nor do you have to purchase piles of tree-killing magazines and cut out your favorite ideas scrapbook-style. You have access to all kinds of ideas on Pinterest for cakes, dresses, invitations, favors, etc. All you need to do is change the boards you are following and add a few of the wedding boards on there. Do I expect you to actually do this? Probably not, but I do encourage you to get involved. If you want to just browse a little, you may see something you think fits with your style and want to put it into your wedding.

Reception Lounge

What is a "reception lounge"? This would be an area separate from the dance floor where guests can mingle, have a beverage or snack, and just step away from the crowd for a minute. A reception lounge can act as sort of a respite from the noise and craziness of the dance floor. You and your bride can feature a special cocktail (named after you, of course) or a few of your other favorite adult beverages. Customize and individualize the lounge by putting some of your favorite songs into a mega-mix to be played at lower volumes so guests are able to actually talk to each other without having to yell over the DJ. Heck, if the reception is overlapping with a must-watch game, feel free to put the game on . . . just kidding, your bride may not be a big fan of that (unless you're *really* lucky). So, unless you clear it with your bride-to-be, don't turn your reception into a sports bar. This will just make the reception itself look like a strange blend of sorority rush and an old-folks home because all the guys will be packed into the new, awesome man cave.

Nuptial Knowledge

Where does the superstition of the groom not seeing the bride on the wedding day come from?

■ It's a carryover from the days of arranged marriages, where the bride and groom had often never seen each other. The thought was, if the groom saw the bride before the wedding and disapproved, he might bolt. Now men are just lucky to sneak a few gifts onto the registry.

Virtual Guests

With today's schedules making life as hectic as ever, this has been a new and growing trend. Impossible even ten years ago, technology has advanced to the point where having virtual guests at your wedding is feasible and even possible financially. You can now have your wedding (you can do the ceremony and reception, but who wants to watch a party they can't attend?) broadcast via the Internet for guests who simply couldn't make it. It isn't as good as attending, but if you have some important people in your life who aren't going to make it, you can always explore this option.

After Party

Throwing an after party following your reception is just like hosting one of the big award shows. It allows everyone to kick off their shoes (not literally, of course), relax, and keep the party rolling. One of the best weddings we went to had an after party at a swanky underground jazz club. It was like a speakeasy at the reception; you know, like, "Pssst—over here. We're ditching Aunt Ethel and the lame guests my mom invited; meet us at the following location." Or better yet, invite Aunt Ethel and Grams—they probably have a little fun left in them.

As the bride and groom, you may not stay long (you've got bigger fish to fry), but your guests will have a great memory of the after party. Plus, whoever is paying for the booze at the reception will thank you for getting everyone to head somewhere else instead of drinking from the wedding bar all night. Also, safety first—many times couples will coordinate some sort of organized transportation to these various locations, so everyone can have a great time and, if they choose to drink, not have to worry.

Keep It Quirky

Somewhere along the way, people realized that if they were going to spend all of this money for a wedding, it might as well be fun. So on the "hot" trend list are things like food truck weddings, circus weddings, and weddings in the park. Out are cheesy DJs and dance floors that remain unoccupied until the last forty-five minutes of the reception when the alcohol kicks in. On-site dance instructors, artists, tarot card readers, and other interactive entertainment are also in. If these kinds of things are affordable for your reception, it makes a lot of sense (and cents!) to use these various forms of entertainment to make your wedding an experience that will be remembered by everyone who attends.

Not Everyone Will Get It

Some of these trends are great and involve an innovative part of your wedding that most people couldn't even have imagined ten years ago. But while this is true, remember that your parents and other family members are from a different generation and it may take a minute for them to accept some of the edgier trends that you and your bride want to incorporate into your special day. But it is *your* wedding, and as long as the quirky trends you adopt for your wedding don't disrupt the key elements of the ceremony, hopefully there won't be too much of a dustup.

Get with the Wedding Program!

- There are traditional duties associated with many key family members, such as the father of the bride, etc. These are good traditions to keep as they let some of the most important people in your lives be involved in the wedding.
- Be very picky about the selection of your best man. You will need someone who will take the role seriously, and act accordingly. He will need to be available to you for some of the wedding planning process, and be there to offer support and advice through the process. It also helps if he can deliver a classic speech!
- Weddings are steeped in tradition. Before you begin to throw them out, look into why they got started in the first place, the meaning behind them, and if this is an element you would like to include in your wedding. Then clear it with your bride!
- Weddings not only involve many traditions, but there are always "hot" trends going on in the world of weddings. These are usually fun, new ideas on ways to perform your wedding reception and ceremony. If you think you and your bride-to-be want to do something trendy and exciting, then go for it! There is no shortage of research to be done.

CHAPTER 5

Make Your Wedding Her Own

It's about time to make some decisions now. You are ready to begin the planning process, but you feel like some wedding traditions are too, well, stuffy to fit your personal style. Well, times are changing (for the better!). What does this mean to you? It means that it's okay to show a little flair and personality in your wedding. If you feel the need to liven it up, well, then go for it! What we will explore in this chapter are some of the popular theme weddings, along with some of the neat little wrinkles couples have created to put their own unique stamp on the proceedings. We know who is getting married, but let's look at the next question: Where?

Your Church or Mine?

If you and your bride are of the same religion, deciding whose church the wedding will be held in is one major decision you can avoid having to navigate. Yes, you might run into some disagreement when deciding whose celebrant will conduct the ceremony, but it is a minor adjustment for the other spouse. However, if you and your BTB hail from different religious backgrounds, you and your fiancée have some decisions to make. So how do you decide in a fair manner whose church the ceremony will take place in and whose religious traditions will be followed?

When it comes to this issue, there are a few choices that come to mind. Either one of you has the option of giving in and crossing over to the other's church for the ceremony. We are talking about the ceremony right now, not long-term life choices. The spouse-to-be that makes this sacrifice may have some explaining to do to his or her family if they are deeply religious. If this is the case, be ready for some "pushback" from the family. By "pushing," I mean anything from screaming and yelling to tears.

So what's behind door number three? If one or the other spouse-to-be either doesn't want to cave in, or the family blowback would just be too much, then you need to get creative. One option is to have celebrants and traditions from both faiths incorporated into a ceremony with multiple celebrants. Don't worry though, you are only married once and will not face polygamy charges. This will appease some of the family and put off the question of faith for you two for a while. Now that you have seen the options for clearing this hurdle, here are some ideas on adding some unique themes into your celebration and/or reception.

For Your Fiancée

I know there is a chance that at this point you are worn out. You have bought an engagement ring, wedding ring, and may be paying for a good bit of the wedding. But I want to encourage you to finish what you started and get your BTB something special as a wedding gift. If you think a wedding is demanding, wait until real life decides to challenge you. So finish what you started and do this right. The gift could be as simple as a special engraving on the inside of her ring that she didn't know you had done. Maybe it's special earrings to wear for the ceremony. Write her a poem or buy her special gear for the honeymoon. Whatever it is, let her know you are all in for the wedding and marriage, with no reservations. Let her know you love her. ■

Types of Weddings

You may be reading along, thinking to yourself, "Hey, I like the idea of a church wedding, but how can we make it more fun?" Lots of couples have had this exact thought and made the decision to spice things up a little bit.

If you are on "Team Traditional" when it comes to your wedding style, then the spice I am referring to may be as simple as special flowers for the wedding or some other small but unique touch that represents your individualism within the framework of a traditional wedding.

If you are thinking of a less traditional style, then feel free to add spice any way you see fit. If you are feeling like you would like to stray from the traditional, but you are unsure in which direction to head, we are going to cover a few ideas to get your brain moving.

Themed

Some of the best events in life are themed. I know I had several superhero-themed birthday parties growing up (usually Batman). Now it seems this idea is catching on with weddings as well. I mean, why not? I had heard that circus weddings were becoming a thing, so I looked to Pinterest (see, I told you it would come in handy). Sure enough, there were couples with wedding pictures with elephants, couples getting married under a red and white striped big top, and bridesmaids with various animal-themed outfits. They even made invitations that looked liked a ticket with the phrase "Admit One." I guess this is the ultimate in fun, where you can spend more or less as your budget calls for and create an unforgettable wedding. It's the perfect "theme" wedding. So if you are thinking that the traditional church wedding lacks enough sizzle for you, go ahead and explore different theme ideas. Here are some other popular themes:

- **Fairy Tale:** Every little girl imagines herself as a princess on her wedding day. Or maybe they don't, I'm not really sure. But if this is a theme that appeals to the two of you, then do it up right. Rent out the finest ballroom in all the land (or neighboring counties), a tiara for the bride, and of course a huge wedding cake. If you really want to carry the theme through, don't forget the horse-drawn carriage to take the happy couple away!

- **Hoedown:** Can you picture it? A beautiful field with horses, maybe even for guests to ride. A red barn that has been cleared (de-smellified?) to allow the proper amount of seating. A parquet dance floor placed on the grass to allow for boot scootin', line dancing, and anything else your guests might be interested in. The fare consists of barbecue, slaw, and any other fixin's you want to put on the menu. Well, if by now you can't picture it, then this theme just isn't for you . . .

- **Active:** Does Red Bull give you wings? Can the two of you just not get enough of the outdoors and all the fun that you can have? Couples like this are creatively incorporating their passion for the outdoors into their wedding. How about you two run a 10k with your guests (those who choose to) and get married at the finish? Why don't you hop on the chair lift and ski into the ceremony? Heck, go ahead and jump out of an airplane and steer your parachute as close as you can to the spot where your guests are waiting.

- **Geek Chic:** Are you guys Trekkies? How about big fans of *Titanic, Star Wars,* or some other classic? What could be more fun than having your reception mirror the alien bar scene in *The Empire Strikes Back*? Sure, these ideas are not for the traditionalist. But if you are looking to go with a really fun theme and one of those movies is on both of your "all-time favorite" lists, then why not? Just make sure the pastor or celebrant is either a Wookiee or Jabba the Hutt.
- **Holiday:** There are so many benefits to planning your wedding around a holiday. First, you have a built-in, fun theme that everyone will go along with. Second, depending on your choice, many holidays have a vacation day associated with them for your guests' convenience. Most importantly, who can forget an anniversary when it is closely tied to a holiday? Even if you grew up Goth, you can go with the month of October and celebrate like it's "Día de los Muertos" or "Day of the Dead." It has nice family-themed elements associated with it. So be creative, and choose the holiday that best represents where you are in your lives. However, as we discussed in Chapter 2, planning a wedding around a holiday may not go over well with some of your guests, so keep that in mind if you choose to run with this theme.

Elope

"Hey, we should just elope!" Ha, ha, ha. Lots of people say this phrase during the wedding planning process. For the uninitiated, eloping is the act of just getting married; there's no fanfare, no reception, no planning. The couple just goes to the justice of the peace and ties the knot. In a way, it makes some sense. Why go through all the pain, heartache, family fights, and cost when there is a simpler solution? Saving tons of cash is the primary reason people decide to elope. After that, the main reasons people elope are to simplify their lives, to avoid fighting with their families, and too much tequila.

Beach Wedding/Destination Wedding

So many couples dream of it; so few really do it. I am not really talking about having your wedding *near* a beach, but having your wedding actually on the beach, sandy feet and all. I am talking about flip-flops or no shoes at all, surf possibly covering you ankle deep, and if you can find one, a steel drum musician providing the ambiance. You can do this but still keep some of the traditional trappings, if you can imagine church with an ocean breeze and a carpet made of sand. This version can be cost-effective, if you are located near a beach to begin with. But if you pick a beach located in the Caribbean, that may not be the case. The exotic beaches also tend to make it difficult to lure lots of guests, as it is expensive for them to travel to your dream destination. But when it's all said and done, who wouldn't smile if they heard "Congratulations, mon!" This really goes for any "destination" wedding you may be considering. Quick tip: Don't forget to check the rules pertaining to obtaining a marriage license in your preferred locale. It varies from city to city, and you don't want to get too far ahead of yourselves, as in, make too many plans before you are sure you can obtain your marriage license in a timely manner.

Home Wedding

Many people with a strong tie to their families and the house they grew up in explore the option of actually getting married in or at that home. It can be nostalgic and charming: Just do not fool yourself into thinking you will be saving boatloads of cash. Don't forget, you will probably want to spruce things up around the house, and you may need to hire a valet service if you don't own six acres in the country, because finding parking for 100 guests will be tricky for most people. Make sure you research all the quirks of having your wedding at home and what that may mean to your budget. For example, you may need to pare down the guest list due to square footage restrictions. You will probably want a caterer, and then you will have strangers roaming your house. But you will save on the venue rental fee! Make sure this is right for both of you before you commit to doing this.

Personalizing Your Day

Just a quick suggestion here to give you a leg up, before we get to the meat and potatoes of the planning process. I know for many men this kind of thing will be counterintuitive. What thing am I referring to? I am speaking of getting really involved in planning the wedding itself.

After all, your wedding is an important event signaling the start of you and your bride's life together. You don't want to be a spectator. So, let's talk about personalizing your wedding and how you can put a little of yourselves into the proceedings.

- **Serve a unique cocktail:** You may want to offer guests a three-ounce cocktail called "The Quickie," while she wants to create a fruity one called "Love Everlasting." Better yet, you could both make up drinks to offer guests and have a blast with it.
- **Make your invitations memorable:** You can add that fun personal touch to your invitations as well. A personal note to the recipient is always a nice touch. Some couples are getting creative by having themed photo shoots beforehand and incorporating the pictures into the invitations.
- **Play your music:** Forget that era of terrible reception music—please, let's forget it. No more "Chicken Dance" or "YMCA." Doctor up a mega-playlist to play while the band takes its break.
- **Introduce a pop of color:** Some couples are having a special wedding color or print that becomes part of the "theme." It doesn't have to be as girly as it sounds. Maybe you get to use camo as the pattern of choice. Camo socks on the groom? Of course, if it ends up being "coral" or "poppy peach," then yeah, it's girly.
- **Design your own wedding cake:** Picking a creative, flexible person to do your wedding cake will allow you to add personality to it. A funny cake topper or a surprising cake color under the outer layer of icing are nice. Then you can always have fun with the groom's cake.

So these are some of the ways you can really add fun and personal touches to different aspects of your big day. In reality, most of these touches do not really cost significantly more to execute, but are more of an expression of your style as a couple. I think it makes couples feel like the wedding is really theirs, as opposed to some predetermined checklist where they are just stand-ins wearing their white dress and tux.

For Your Fiancée

Sometimes you need to throw aside the instincts that tell you that you do not care about some of the finer details of the wedding experience. If it matters to your bride-to-be, then it will begin to matter to you. So start a "wedding book" for right after the engagement to give to her. You can do it old-school with a binder and a truckload of magazines to look through, or create an electronic one online. Spend some time putting together a few simple ideas you like to start the process. It doesn't matter if they all get discarded later. She will be thrilled you are putting in some time and effort, showing you are excited about your wedding. ■

Venue and Menu

Selecting your menu and venue are very important, and you need to think it through a little bit to allow you to do it right, a.k.a. your way. Adding these touches of personal style to the venue are key, because it is a visual representation of your theme and personality. It is a huge way for you to imprint your taste on the proceedings, and it will be memorable for the guests as well.

Venue

We talked about choosing your venue back in Chapter 2, but here we'll go over how to make sure that venue seems special to you, your bride-to-be, and your guests. The correct venue will be in sync with your theme, make an impression with your guests, and most importantly, be available for the date of your wedding. How can you take your venue and make it special? Well . . .

- **Get Those Chair Covers:** Okay, it seems like a small thing, but trust me, it will make a difference—especially for your bride-to-be! Chair covers are just fabric covers that you (or the manager of the your venue) will throw over the boring chairs in your hall. These covers can add the color and sense of style that you and your bride-to-be are really shooting for.
- **Flowers and Decorations:** The floral decorations and other decor pieces you choose will help transform your venue from a room with folding chairs arranged around card tables into something special. You want to give a certain look and feel to your proceedings so the guests have a fun, unique experience.
- **Show a Photo Slideshow:** One fun element may be to create a slideshow of pictures of the happy couple. Dig deep and include pictures of the two of you when you were young all the way to the present time. It's a way for the guests and family to be entertained and see you at various times in your lives. If you really want to spice it up, and don't mind a little extra work, have someone snap photos during the pre-wedding and reception. You can upload them in real time if you want to!
- **Move the Tables:** Get a little creative with the tables and how you set them up. A long rectangle at the front of the room for the wedding party is always fun, and that way all the guests can see what you are up to. Mixing shapes and sizes can add to the overall eclectic feel of the reception.

- **Light It Up:** If you have extra budget (or just a large one), spend a few bucks to get professional lighting done. You can highlight the parts of a room you love while you minimize others. You can change the lighting when it's time to relax, when it's time to party, and then bring the lights up when it's time to go.

Weddings are never about the bride and groom, weddings are public platforms for dysfunctional families.

—Lisa Kleypas, author

As you figure out how to personalize your venue, keep your time in mind. For example, if you come up with a great strategy that involves you making favors for 100 guests, sewing your own dress, and making special playlists for the reception, you are going to be busy. Besides, even if you have the talent to be a DJ, wedding planner, cake decorator, and seamstress, are you sure you have time to do it *all*? There is an entire industry built up around people who perform these functions, and it may be a better idea for you to direct them rather than try to replace them.

Menu
Now that we are making progress on creating a venue that feels right, let's turn to the menu. Chicken and prime rib, with a chocolate fountain, right? Well, that's one option. You can also personalize the proceedings to help make even the meal more fun for everyone. Naming the different menu choices in sections of the buffet after you and the bride is silly and fun. You can also serve a special dish

from an old family recipe or from the first date you went on with your BTB.

But as you make your day special, it is also important to think about your menu in terms of your guests and your venue—and don't forget your budget! Do any guests need a special menu provided? Are there any food allergies that you need to watch out for? These are the kinds of considerations you need to take into account when planning out the foods you will be serving.

Nuptial Knowledge

Why do the bride and groom cut the wedding cake together?

■ This is symbolic of the joining of their lives and a life together going forward.

Incorporating Your Families

If you are lucky, there are people in your life that you refer to as your "loved ones." And, if you are really, really lucky, you like your fiancée's family and she likes yours. Now take a quick second and go buy a lottery ticket, because many couples have individuals in their respective families that they wish they could get away with not inviting to the wedding. Worse yet, some of those infamous "black sheep" will be mingling with your friends and her friends—hopefully not doing things that embarrass you. Hopefully the damage will be minimal, and your uncle will keep his pants on as the evening progresses. That said, let's take a look at some of the family members who will almost certainly be there, whatever your opinion of them, and what roles they may play in your wedding. Just on a final note, you have taken the first step of including family by inviting them. Now give them something to do. They are cheap labor and incorporating them into the proceedings will make it special for them—and your BTB—as well.

Grandparents

You have a few options on how to handle your grandparents, depending on your family. If your grandparents are still with us, you could have a special procession where all of the ushers lead them into the ceremony venue right before the ceremony starts, which will draw lots of fuss and attention to them. Many couples have their grandparents wear flowers, and remember to give them special thanks in the wedding program. Prod your bride to ask the grandmothers—both yours and hers—for the "something borrowed" or "something old" that she'll want to incorporate into her wedding attire, to make sure they know how special they are to both of you. Also, if your grandparents have been married for what seems like forever, honoring them at your reception is always nice. You could say something like, "We look to our grandparents for inspiration because they have been married for forty-seven years . . ." You can write this into the program, or leave a card at each reception table if you want.

If you are trying to incorporate and honor deceased grandparents, you can certainly find a way to do their memory justice. Here are some of the best ideas floating around out there:

- **Symbolic flower:** Leaving a symbolic flower in the seat where your grandparent may have been seated during the ceremony is a nice way to honor his or her memory.
- **Picture:** Many brides, paying a more private tribute to a deceased loved one, will carry a picture of their loved one in a brooch or placed amongst their flowers.

- **Reserve a seat in his or her memory:** Both at the ceremony and at the reception, couples will reserve a seat for a grandparent who has passed, with a picture of something to remember him or her by. They will usually place a card stating that the seat is reserved "In memory of . . ."
- **Take a moment of silence:** To honor your grandparents, you can observe a public moment of silence for all of your guests to share, or you and your fiancée can share a special moment of silence just before you enter the church. I like this more as a part of the ceremony, when a solemn moment will be more in line with the tone of the proceedings.

There are a lot of ways to honor your grandparents. What matters is that you honor them the way you feel is best.

Nuptial Knowledge

Why do guests traditionally throw rice at the newly married couple?

■ Rice is thrown at the newlyweds because it is a traditional symbol of fertility and blessing for prosperity. However, it has been shown to harm birds if not cleaned up promptly, so more recent alternatives include blowing bubbles or tossing rose petals at the new couple.

Siblings

In times long ago, it could be a challenge to incorporate siblings into your wedding. If, say, your BTB had a brother or two that you had only met once or twice and didn't really know that well, you'd probably be wondering if you really wanted to make him a groomsman. If your bride only had four bridesmaids, you certainly wanted to choose people close to you, not long lost relatives who you barely had any connection with. But this was more of a problem, in my eyes, back when we were slaves to tradition. Times have changed so much, and somewhere along the way people stopped following tradition just for the sake of tradition. Today, you can call for an even trade if you both have the same number of opposite sex siblings. They will effectively cancel each other out, not taking up slots that could be filled by close friends. If you have a gaggle of siblings, just have them symbolically in the wedding party and all walk down the aisle before the rest of the wedding party and take their reserved seats near the front. This will allow you to include all kinds of family, yet ensure that you have room for your close friends as well.

Kids

If either you or your fiancée has children, they should most definitely be involved in the proceedings. The most prominent choice for kids tends to either be as a flower girl or as a ring bearer. I have also heard the idea (and approve) that if the bride has children, you should have them "give her away" to the groom as a symbol of their approval of the union. Other ideas include:

- **Have kids say "I do."** This is a nice way to include the children. It's simple and yet symbolic where they are accepting the formation of their new family.
- **Present kids with a special gift as part of the ceremony.** You know, bribe them! Actually, it is an appropriate gesture, as they will see all of the gifts you and your BTB receive, and you want them to feel

special and that they are part of the proceedings in
their own way.

- **Write vows to the children that are read during
  the ceremony.** This can be cute and will give the
  kids their part. As a parent, you or your BTB must
  decide if this will be more stressful or embarrassing
  for them and weigh that against the value of them
  taking part in the ceremony.

- **Have the officiant bless the family as a group at
  the end of the ceremony (especially for religious
  ceremonies).** Depending on the children's ages, they
  may or may not understand what is happening or the
  meaning of this blessing. But it is a nice sentiment to
  have a blessing placed on the new family.

- **Have the children (if old enough) light the unity
  candle with you and your bride.** This will make
  them feel included and part of the ceremony. Just
  make sure they're old enough to be walking around
  with lit candles.

It is important to incorporate the children as part of the
wedding. The marriage will all be new to them, and it gets
the new family off to a great start if everyone is excited about
the wedding and the part they play in it. So work with your
kids (or hers) to find them a role that they are excited about!

Pets

Pets are a big part of many people's lives, and they are a
part of the family. Today, some couples are even giving their
special pets a part to play in the wedding.

- **Ring Bearer:** As with young children, Scruffy will not actually be transporting the expensive rings down the aisle. Pets can easily get distracted with all of the new faces in the crowd, and losing the rings would be a disaster! For pets, they usually carry a pillow with false rings strapped to it in the cameo role as "ring bearer."
- **Guest of Honor:** You can have your pet sit off to the side like a mascot at a college football game, symbolically blessing the proceeding with his presence. You may need to hire a pet sitter to keep an eye on your dog during the time he will be there.
- **Picture This:** Some couples choose to include their pet in the photo sessions. Couples have gotten cute photos of their pet and used these on table cards or rehearsal dinner invitations. If your pet will cooperate, your can give him a matching bow tie or give her a sparkling tiara.

Just keep in mind your pet's personality when you do this. If they are easily scared or aggressive toward strangers, then it may be best to let sleeping dogs lie and include the pets in your lives and not your wedding.

So there you have it. It is easy on one hand: Think of all of the people and family (even pets!) who make your life special. Then find creative ways to include them in the proceedings. It will mean a lot to them that you thought of them. If you come up with a role for a family member you aren't sure that person wants to do, just ask him or her.

Get with the Wedding Program!

- If you come from different religious backgrounds, there can be difficulty honoring all of the traditions and keeping the respective families at peace. The two of you need to come to one opinion on these issues and present a united front to your respective families.
- While you are having all of these meaningful discussions, go ahead and decide what type of wedding you are having. Is it reverent and traditional? Are you going to be emphasizing a certain theme?
- Whatever style wedding you choose, add some of your own personality to it. Even minor touches that display your personal style and personality will make the wedding more meaningful and memorable.
- If you have a great relationship with your family, they will love you and appreciate it so much if you can find a role for them to play in the wedding.
- There are many ways to honor important people from your life that have passed away. Reserving a special spot for them at the ceremony or having a keepsake with you that reminds you of them are both ways to honor your lost loved ones.
- Children and your special pets are a part of your new family, so why not include them? Especially with children, it is nice to give them a role to play to make them feel a part of the proceedings.

CHAPTER 6

Put the Party in Wedding Party

If you are not sure what a wedding party is yet, now is the time to figure it out. Although your wedding can be a fun party, and your wedding party can party, neither of those descriptions is accurate. The wedding party consists of you, the bride, and the bridesmaids and groomsmen you have selected. In most cases, the number of bridesmaids and groomsmen are the same, leading to a nice symmetry for the entrance to the ceremony and reception, and it's good for pictures also. So, in this chapter, we'll go over the role each member of your wedding party needs to play, how to select the members of your wedding party, and what you need to give them as a thank-you when all is said and done.

Selecting Your Best Man

How do you go about selecting this "best man"? We alluded to the important criteria earlier. He needs to be someone who you both respect and enjoy spending time with. Someone mature enough to give a credible speech and to know what is inbounds for the bachelor party—and strong enough to throw a flag if things are headed off course. Most importantly, he must be someone who will be on time to the wedding-related events. It's worth repeating: Whether or not your best man is naturally inclined to be responsible, you will need him to be very punctual. Nothing will irritate you faster than to have to wait on a tardy best man or groomsmen. Trust me on this one. Now, it may seem like I just described either your father or a big brother—and many a groom have used these people in this role—but most of the time the best man is a friend who is so close that he is like a brother. Someone who will gladly fill this role and do so capably out of respect for the friendship the two of you share. If you have a brother, then so much the better. Sign him up! Unless you guys are long lost siblings or are just simply on bad terms, use family. They will be with you the rest of your life.

My paralyzing fear of giving best man speeches prevents me from being anyone's closest friend.
—Unknown author

It's okay to talk to your best man after he accepts the responsibility to map out some of the requirements that you will place on him for the role. If the time commitment is too burdensome or he will not be able to fulfill his role due to other commitments (such as work), then it's better to know this up front, before you start getting close to the magic date and wondering to yourself, "Why in the hell didn't he tell me he couldn't make half the planning events?" And you will want him to be involved in some of the planning, even if it is just to tag along and learn the schedule of events, meet some of the family, and learn about the wedding itself. Guests will be going to members of the wedding party with questions from "Why did they pick this as their signature cocktail?" to "Where is the restroom?" and the more involved he is in the planning, the more he will be at the ready to help. Unfortunately, that being said, there is a logistical aspect to this process. It will be really hard to involve a best man who lives out of town. You can do it, and the extra work you'll do to keep him informed will be worth it if he is the guy for the job. But it's better to have a best man who can make most of the appointments.

What else will your best man have to do? We have hinted and teased at some of his responsibilities along the way, but we will take a deeper look here:

Nuptial Knowledge

True or False: Bachelor parties were started by the Spartans.

■ It's true. Spartan soldiers began giving grooms a boys-only party similar to the night before a huge battle. No word on whether they were meaning to compare the two events.

Bachelor Party

If you have a taste for such things, I have heard of this city in the desert that is sort of built around the idea of total irresponsibility. I think it's called Las something or other . . . Vegas, maybe? Yes, fabulous Las Vegas. If you and your fellow groomsmen decide you simply cannot resist the "One Last Blast" idea (this was also my high school graduation theme), then by all means help yourself. Just remember, there is a reason they set the film *The Hangover* there, and you don't want to end up with a face tattoo, a pet tiger, or the most likely scenario, empty pockets except for a mountain of ATM withdrawal receipts.

While *The Hangover* was fun to watch, when it comes to the bachelor party, my advice here is to not tempt fate. Maybe I have seen too many movies where these parties go bad, but I would advise you to make sure your best man keeps it "classy." Trust me, it's for your own good!

We go into the bachelor party in more detail in Chapter 9, but once you figure out what kind of bachelor party you really want, it is up to your best man to put your wishes into action. He needs to clear potential dates with you, and clear the guest list, unless there are a few "surprise" guests he may include. I've been a surprise guest, and it was quite fun to pop out from behind a slot machine and see the look on my friend's face. Your best man doesn't have to give you many details, but let him know if there are any "must-haves" for you.

Fittings

The best man is required to rent and wear the appointed tux or suit that you, the groom, request him to wear. He should also help wrangle the other groomsmen to do this as well in a timely manner. The "fitting" I refer to is the adjustment the tuxedo providers make to help the tux fit each individual. Out-of-town groomsmen can go to any tux shop near them and get measured. They'll send the measurements to you for when you pick out the groomsmen's uniform. Then, as early as possible, get your groomsmen to try on their garb. The tux shop can make adjustments as needed, and everyone will look sharp for your big day.

Wedding Rehearsal and Rehearsal Dinner

The day before the wedding, there will be a ceremony rehearsal, where you will go through where everyone stands, where they need to be at any given time during the proceedings, as well as practice everyone's entrance and exit. Readers will be given their cues as well. Not every best man is built this way, but it is great if he can pay close attention and keep everyone in line. Then when the wedding arrives, he can help those who forget where they're supposed to be (there is always at least one who does) be where they should be and keep the ceremony running smoothly.

As for the rehearsal dinner, the best man will attend and be friendly and accommodating to the other guests. He may be asked to give some sort of toast, but since he will be on the big stage for his toast at the reception, he may want to keep it short and sweet. At this particular event, the father of the groom and even the bride's father like to get their licks in, so he may not be called upon. You and your BTB can talk about this beforehand. The dads may feel like they want the mic, so to speak, to welcome everyone and say a few words about the happy couple. Get with your BTB and see how planned out you want to make it, or if you just want to go with the flow.

At the Ceremony

The morning of the ceremony, the best man will be busy. He will be your support, your gopher, and basically your manservant. Why do his duties include getting you anything and everything you need? It's because you may be nervous and will be focusing on the wedding itself. At this point, anything your best man can do to calm you down is exactly what he should do. In addition, if you are experiencing any last-second doubts, he either needs to support or encourage you, or find someone who can. This is where he earns the better gift than the rest of the groomsmen. I suggest involving other family or friends as ushers to help seat guests. Then the best man can hang out with you, help you get your tie just right, and help keep things light as time ticks away up to the ceremony.

At the Reception

Usually couples will make a grand entrance to the reception, and the wedding party will be introduced as well. Your BMF (best man forever) will escort in the maid of honor, and the rest will be paired off for symmetry. You should be able to count on your best man to wrangle the other groomsmen for pictures, decorate your getaway car, etc. All of these things are important. But once you get into the reception . . .

Well, now it's your best man's time to shine. It's time for his big speech, the best man's toast. Now, he will need to do some sort of preparation for this—and you may need to do some preparation as well. If there is any doubt in your mind concerning your best man's judgment about what is appropriate for inclusion in his speech, have a little man-to-man chat with him ahead of time and respectfully ask him to omit the story about the time you donned wood shop goggles, rubber kitchen gloves, and a bike helmet and decided to see how long you could hold on to the roof of a speeding car. Your short-lived career in the "reverse auto-luge" doesn't really need to be discussed with your family—or hers. I've always felt that it's a good idea to focus on the groom's more positive traits, and I'm sure you'd agree. Although it seems obvious to me that this is the way to play the best man speech, I have attended a wedding where the best man, I suppose as some form of frontier justice or gamesmanship, decided to tell a particularly sordid story about the groom's past romantic exploits. As the tale became more sordid and graphic, everyone (including the pastor) became more uncomfortable by the minute. To exacerbate the situation, one of the groomsmen misread the situation and decided he *had* to tell a story that was even better. And by better, I mean worse. So as the groom, it may not be appropriate to write your own speech, but a little best man coaching never hurt.

Post-Ceremony

The best man gets all sorts of fun jobs after the festivities end. He should recruit a team to make sure everyone is getting home safely from the reception. He can go through the reception area to ensure no valuables were left behind. He will probably be in charge of getting your tux back to the shop the next day if you rented. He should also help you handle the caterers and the DJ/band, and should hand out any tips per your instructions (after all, you provide the funds for tips, not him!). This is another spot where his responsibility level can be key. You don't want him too focused on making time with the bridesmaids to remember to pass out the tips or return the tux.

Thank Him!

After he commits all of this time and effort to being a model best man, it is another tradition (and simply a nice thing to do) to give him a gift to thank him for all his efforts. You'll want to give gifts to your groomsmen too, but typically you'd go with a common gift for them and some sort of superior gift for the best man. It might be nice to give them something fun to commemorate the wedding weekend! Depending on your budget it can be excellent beer steins, poker cards with your face in different poses, or simply a bottle of wine from dinner the night before (or one you really like). Again, whatever you decide to give, make sure to pump the best man's gift up a few notches. After all, if he has done his job correctly, he's gone far above the rest of the groomsmen. Just so we are clear, I'm not advising getting the groomsmen all six-packs of beer, while the best man takes home a "twelver." I hope you can do better than that.

Groomsmen Selection and Responsibilities

Okay, when you sit down to decide on your groomsmen, you can just pick anyone you want and expect that to be okay with your bride-to-be, right? Not so much. Your fiancée will most likely tell you how many people you need to recruit for your part of the wedding party. Most ceremonies cry out for symmetry, and unless one of your groomsmen is going to be carrying a virtual bridesmaid who is FaceTiming into the wedding on an iPad, you will be allotted a groomsmen number to match the number of bridesmaids. That way each of your groomsmen will have a partner to enter and exit the ceremony with, and this also allows everyone to pair off for the ceremonial dance.

Selecting Your Groomsmen

So who should you select as groomsmen? Most friends will know if they are in the running for best man or not, but everyone from your out-of-town cousin to your lab partner from high school may consider themselves in the running for a groomsman spot. If your wedding looks like it's going to be especially fun, then they will be jockeying even harder.

So, who are the finalists? I recommend selecting your groomsmen from a group of your close friends who didn't make the best man spot, and I am always in favor of incorporating a family member whenever possible. Just remember, by selecting someone to be a groomsman, you are, in a way, cementing the bond between the two of you for a long time to come. I mean, you could have just about anyone stand there in a tux, but when it is a close friend or relative who you have a relationship with, it becomes special. Also, if you have a friendship that has been fading from sight for a while, think about whether this is just due to circumstances or if you think it is just a bump in the road before asking that person to be in your party. You would prefer someone who cares about you and is willing and enthusiastic to perform his duties. You don't need someone who could care less, or is only halfheartedly participating.

For Your Fiancée

You can help your bride-to-be include the important male members of her family in the wedding with a little bit of negotiation. For example, if your fiancée has a brother who she wants to include, feel free to have him as a groomsman. But turnaround is fair play here, and your bride-to-be should be ready to take in a bridesmaid of your choosing (your sister, close friend, etc.) as part of the deal. In today's world, you and your bride-to-be can even buck tradition and have a close female relative stand with you and your bride's brother stand on her side. ■

Groomsmen Gifts

Believe it or not, groomsmen usually get gifts as well, which is just a bonus to something that's already a pretty sweet deal. It is not a bad job if you get to go to the bachelor party, escort a pretty girl down the aisle, and then hang out at the reception and throw a few waters back. Not a bad way to pass a weekend. As for the gifts for these clowns, simple and classic goes a long way. A particularly unique set of wine glasses or beer steins may be a possibility, or a framed picture of all of you from the bachelor party may be nice. Don't worry about a gift's monetary value here; it is more about how the unique nature of the gifts can represent some shared experience than how much the gift may cost.

The Ring Bearer

Usually a young person with close ties to you and your fiancée performs the role of ring bearer. The ring bearer can be a boy or girl, and if there are two ideal candidates, they can hold the rings together and present them for the ceremony. The main qualifications for this position are being close to the families, being under the age of eight, and being really cute. Just so you know, it is by no means mandatory for you to have a ring bearer at your ceremony, especially if you have a lot of nephews and are worried about hurt feelings. If you decide to incorporate a younger child, let that child know he or she is really helping you out. Maybe you can keep one of the ring bearer's parents on alert in case the child is overcome with shyness and needs a little help. Before you start wondering if you should trust a child to balance an expensive ring on a pillow while walking up the aisle, don't fret. Often a "dummy" ring is used, not the real thing. It is just a way to add some youth and innocence to the proceedings and make the child feel special.

Get with the Wedding Program!

- For you, selecting the best man is an important task. He will have many responsibilities if he is doing his job correctly, and you want someone who will be a positive factor, not someone who adds stress to the day. You may even want to discuss some of the responsibilities with him to make sure he can follow through.

- When it comes to the bachelor party, make sure you are on the same page as your best man. Although he will be planning the occasion, he should respect your wishes as to what type of event you want and if there is anyone you especially want to invite. Remember, you are not going off to war. Just doing something fun as a group will be great (i.e. don't do anything stupid!).

- The groomsmen field will include other close friends and family. If you need to trade a groomsman position for the bride's brother so your sister can be included as a bridesmaid, that works. You will probably be limited to matching the number of groomsmen you have to the number of bridesmaids. It gives symmetry to the proceedings.

- It is a great gesture to get a gift for your best man (and groomsmen) if possible. Something personalized or linked to your ceremony or bachelor event is a fun way to add meaning to the gift.

- If you have that special nephew, let him be the ring bearer for the ceremony. It is special for him and adds a note of innocence and youth to your wedding.

CHAPTER 7

Wardrobe and Accessories

You may not really follow the world of fashion. You may not care too much about what you wear on a daily basis, either. But while your clothes may not matter much when you are mowing the yard, when you are dedicating your life to your BTB in front of all of your friends and family, you might as well look nice while you do it. Yes, I know you can run down to the tux store, get the James Bond special, and be in and out of there in a few minutes. But don't you want to do something a little more fun? Here, we'll look at some of the options available to you, some of the styles and looks you can try. We will take a look at how to outfit your groomsmen and figure out the whole ring selection process. We have a lot to cover, so let's get started.

Dressing for the Occasion

If the old saying "the clothes make the man" holds true in your mind, then you may be feeling a little pressure while figuring out what exactly to wear on what is commonly thought of as one of the most important days in a man's life. It isn't like prom, where you and your "bros" donned a '70s-style electric blue ruffled tux. That won't fly here, unless you are having a throwback wedding. Just in case you want to put a little more thought into it—which your bride-to-be will likely appreciate—we will go over some of the basic options to give you a little food for thought on what you might like to wear on your wedding day.

So assuming you are not going with a simple penguin suit, let's look at some ideas and options. There are so many more interesting ways that you can express yourself today, why would you want to play it conservative?

Nuptial Knowledge

When and where did the tradition of a white wedding dress get started?

■ It's rumored that the tradition of the white dress began in 1840 when Queen Victoria wore a white dress. Before that time, brides just wore their "Sunday best."

Rent or Buy?

Are you going to rent or purchase a tux? That is the first thing you need to figure out, and there are pluses and minuses for both options. If you buy a tux, you guarantee that you'll get married in a well-fitting, custom tux that matches your style to a T; you won't have to choose from whatever the tux store has on hand. Also, you get to keep the tux after the wedding, so as long as you don't undergo severe weight loss or gain, you will be covered for those times when formal dress is required.

The main negative to purchasing a tux is the cost. You may end up paying three to four times more to purchase your tux than to simply rent one. Take a realistic look at your wallet and your lifestyle and see what makes sense. You could always ask for season tickets to the symphony orchestra as a wedding gift to ensure that you will have an opportunity to wear it often.

The advantages of renting are many, and that's why so many go this route. Generally, if you are wearing a tux with "flair" or a special color, you may not want to keep this look in the long term. Also, when you rent a tux, the store is usually nice enough to include shoes, vest, tie, etc., in the rental cost. If you are buying your tux, you will probably have to buy these items separately.

To Bow Tie or Not to Bow Tie

First you will need to figure out what your outfit for the big day will be, then it's time to ask yourself if you are going to wear a bow tie or neck tie. Do your homework and look at various examples of wedding attire for men. Some styles complement different body types, so maybe you want to flatter yourself as much as possible.

Once you have it figured out, go ahead and learn how to tie a tie if you don't already know. Think of it as a rite of passage. The Sateré-Mawé tribe of the Amazon region force their young men to repeatedly place their hands into gloves filled with venomous ants to prove their manhood. The least you can do is learn to tie your own bow tie (and tie!). If you are clueless on how to do this, there are a myriad of videos and illustrations available online. But I did find a couple of useful tips while asking around to those oh-so dedicated bow tie wearers:

- If you are struggling with the diagrams, it is similar to tying your shoe. If you can't tie your own shoes, well, then we have a whole other problem to discuss.
- Once you have the basics down, try tying your bow tie in different sizes and vary the angle of the tie. It is the little ways that you express yourself that make a difference.
- Above all else, your tie should be comfortable and allow blood to flow freely. You will be wearing this tie for several hours after all.

Keep in mind that some of the rental ties sometimes have more of a fastening clasp as opposed to a full on bow tie you tie yourself. If you happen to be taking a stab at being fashionable with a regular tie of some sort, learn that process as well. You never know when it will come in handy.

Don't Wear a Cummerbund

Seriously. Don't wear a cummerbund or anything that needs to stay on with the use of Velcro. The cummerbund had its day, its time in the sun. It's time we retire it and move forward. If you are going to go for an elegant, traditional look, then keep it clean and elegant instead of "dressing it up" with something that is like a stain-resistant WWE belt. While general men's "formalwear" stores still push it, more modern men's guides have pronounced it dead. If you have your heart set on it, I guess nobody would outright laugh at you, but there are so many better options available to you, like a vest or braces that can add a layer of sophistication to your look.

For Your Fiancée

When it comes time to pick your attire for the wedding, make sure you are consulting your BTB. You want your suit to be in lockstep with her dress, and that includes what level of formality you are both selecting. I know to some of us, all tuxes and wedding gowns are the same. But this is not really the case, and your suit needs to match her dress in style and how formal it is. If you walk into the tux shop and they ask about what your bride is wearing, it is because they are trying to help you achieve this. So plan with your BTB to make sure you are on the same page. ■

Own Your Outfit

Okay, I don't literally mean "own"; we covered that earlier in this chapter. However, you do want to make sure that you feel great in whatever you're wearing, and you should feel free to spice up your clothes for your wedding day.

After all, when you wear something more than the simple tux, you are trying to go from simply looking "nice" to attempting to look something closer to "dashing." You will feel better as well, because you have made the outfit your own. And above all else, even though your bride-to-be will be the shining star, you and your groomsmen do not need to be simply window dressing. You are men, and you should dress appropriately. This means that matching the groomsmen's vests to the brightly colored bridesmaids' dresses does not cut the mustard. Instead, it turns your men into human accessories to the bride and her friends. So whatever you wear, bear in mind that you are there to be a strong, elegant, and masculine backdrop to the bride's shining star, not an extension of her and her bridesmaids' attire.

So what can you do to own the outfit, without looking like you're trying to scream for attention or compete with your bride? Let's look at some basic information you'll need to make your outfit your own.

Time of Wedding

The time of your ceremony will be the first dictator of your outfit choice. Generally speaking, the traditional black tux is for evening wear. Wearing black during a sunny day can make you look washed out at best, or at worst a simple black suit can make guests think you are in mourning. When you are holding the ceremony in the daytime, you must dress accordingly. So we will take our cue from centuries of tradition here. Take a long look at the "morning dress," as the Brits often call it. There will be someone to assist you in your selection at the formalwear shop, but here are a few guidelines:

- Dark gray or black jacket
- Gray or black pants (In the world of formalwear, these are often called *trousers*. May I recommend just one pleat?)
- Light-colored vest (a chance to personalize the outfit)
- Formal necktie (another chance for you to pick something you like)
- White shirt (sorry, no electric blue)
- Black oxford shoes (no wingtips)

Even if this sounds a bit prohibitive, "morning dress" does give you the opportunity to accessorize your outfit with other appropriate additions:

- Cufflinks (Guys, we do not get a lot of options, but here is a small one. Cufflinks can be traditional or fun. The only real guideline here is they should coordinate with the style of jewelry that your bride has selected.)
- A single flower (from the bride's flowers is one idea)
- Watch (or pocket watch)

This is a classic look that at least allows you a few choices to help make it your own. It is often seen in pictures with a top hat. Keep in mind that not a lot of guys can pull off the top hat without looking a bit foolish. But if you can, then by all means go for it.

If you are holding an evening ceremony, then the game changes. The color black is the color for an evening wedding for oh so many reasons. First, black is the color of the night. Whereas a black tux may look faded and wash out your face during a bright sunny day, it represents strength, elegance, and maybe even a touch of mystery during an evening event. Also, as we briefly discussed, part of the function of the groom is to be a simple backdrop for the bride. Black provides a nice background for the bride to shine, as it is her show. This is both conceptual, as you are allowing your bride to shine, and literal, as it will help make for better wedding photos.

Dare to Be Different

Today's groom is less bound by tradition, and many men are finding that there are many ways to look stylish besides putting on the traditional penguin suit. If you want to bow out of formalwear, today it's acceptable to opt for more casual and stylish options, like a finely tailored suit. You could even split the difference by wearing a tuxedo suit paired with a skinny tie. If done correctly, all of these looks can keep you looking like a groom, just a groom that was born after 1990. In addition, some of today's grooms are following these newly emerging wedding trends:

- **Patterned Suits:** Mostly these are semiformal. They can run from eye-catching stripes to flamboyant checks. This is probably only an option if it fits with the rest of your theme.
- **Brightly Colored Socks:** A fun little touch. You can coordinate with something of the bride's, your "wedding color," or the bridesmaids' dresses. You can even do something all your own here, because as long as your pants fit, then your fun socks shouldn't distract from the proceedings.
- **Sneakers:** My first reaction is just . . . don't. But after some extensive Googling, I realized that this look can actually be pulled off pretty well. Yes, if there are older gentlemen in the wedding party, chances are they will need to take a moment to themselves to adjust to this idea. But however you handle this idea, try to shoot for a unique, fun look and not a shabby, underdressed, look.
- **Brightly Colored Tie:** This can be fun, as it adds some color to the proceedings. If you go down this road, look for something the bride is wearing or play off the colors of the flowers in her bouquet.
- **Go Traditional:** Today, we are seeing some grooms rock a cultural vibe with a kilt or robe from their family background. If you feel strongly about your culture—or hers—feel free to try out some more traditional garb.

No matter what you choose to wear, your attire for this most important day must be a function of time of day, how formal the event is, and of course that personal style or expression that can make something your own.

For Your Fiancée:

It is time your entered into the next level of manhood. Time for one of those traditions handed down from father to son. Time to learn about your BTB's wedding dress. Those fancy dresses that will make your BTB look on special on the big day are often made of layers and layers of fabrics. The style, cut, and season are just some of the factors that play into what fabrics should be included in the dress. They range from ones you have heard of, like polyester and silk, to ones you may not have heard of, like brocade, georgette, and moiré. The fabrics that you haven't heard of tend to be more expensive as well. Other factors that may affect your budget include the designer of the dress. Beautiful gowns can be had anywhere from under $1,000 all the way up. If you as a couple are going to pay several thousand dollars for your BTB's dress, make sure she is getting the good stuff and not just polyester. ■

Outfitting Your Groomsmen

So while your wife is the belle of the ball, so to speak, and you're dressing to be the best in show (men's category), you have the power to dress your groomsmen. And with great power comes great responsibility. You can be open to opinions and ideas, but ultimately the choice of what your best man and groomsmen wear will be yours. Remember, as we touched on earlier, neither you nor your groomsmen should act as living accessories to the bride or her party. While it is okay to coordinate the overall level of formality along with thematic concerns, you are not there to look like your bride's handbag and neither are your friends.

When you are deciding how to dress the groomsmen, think about it as if you are the king, and they are your court. So when you take a look at your ensemble, consider the fact that your groomsmen will always look just a step below. For example, if you decide to go with the formal single-breasted jacket, you may have your groomsmen go with the slightly less formal version or a double-breasted jacket. You may wear the more formal white waistcoat, while they sport the less formal (but very traditional) black version. I think you are getting the general idea here. Many of these things will depend on the same factors we mentioned before: the season, style, and time of day of the ceremony.

Best Man Versus Groomsmen

Now that you've put all of this effort into choosing your tux, you don't want to look just like your grooms-men. Ideally you would structure your groom's "look" with some options. Some grooms choose to create three "tiers": one for the groom, then the best man in a just slightly different version of the same outfit, and then the grooms-men with just a few modifications to differentiate, but still mostly the same look. It seems fitting to make the best man stand out slightly with a different boutonniere or a symbol so that when everyone lines up, there is a visual component to the hierarchy.

Wedding Rings

We talked briefly about budgeting for your and your bride-to-be's rings in Chapter 3, but here we'll dive deeper into how you go about choosing a piece of jewelry that you'll be wearing for (if you're lucky) the rest of your life. Yes, we're talking about the all-important wedding ring. What should you focus on as you shop? Here are some shopping tips you can keep in mind when running out to the local jeweler:

Keep It Coordinated

The first criterion you should have for the wedding rings is to make sure that there's some sort of theme or coordination between the rings for you and your bride. At least they can be made out of the same metal (gold, platinum, etc.). They don't have to be totally matchy-matchy, but if they are so far apart that they don't look like they belong in the same room together, then if nothing else they will make for a lousy picture of your two hands clasped together in the wedding album . . . that and your hairy fingers.

Nuptial Knowledge

Why are wedding rings worn on the third finger of the left hand?

■ Egyptians believed the vein in that finger ran directly to the heart.

Be Narrow-Minded

If you are not a shopper at heart, there are some decisions that the two of you can determine that will narrow the field before you ever get in the car to head out shopping. Figure out if you are going white, yellow, or platinum. Real or cubic zirconia? Colored accent stones or not? You can look at almost endless examples of different ideas on the Internet before you go, and then get a price range for the various differences. If the engagement ring comes with a coordinated wedding ring option, you can check it out, but feel free to simply pick your own out instead—and let your BTB do the same.

Start Early

You may want to only have to go out shopping one time, but you would hate to be forced into making this large and important purchase under pressure. Conceivably you could be wearing this ring for the rest of your life, so you better take the time to find one that you like. Try putting some real time and effort into this as far ahead of the wedding date as possible. Look online, then go to local stores. You should know what you are looking for, but keep an open mind. Astute readers will be asking how this works with my advice above about keeping a "narrow" focus. What I mean here is that know what you want and do your home-work, but if you get to the store and see a totally new design idea you never knew existed, then be open to it. Or maybe you get to the store and the ring just doesn't look right on your finger. Well, if you start out far enough ahead, then you will be able to change course if needed. You should also be ready and able to buy, but you do not want to make a rushed purchase because you waited too long and the wedding is fast approaching. If you look in enough places, you may just find your dream ring on budget where and when you least expect it.

Make Sure the Price Is Right

Again, we discussed budgeting for your ring in Chapter 3, but whatever you spend, you need to make sure the price is right. This refers to the game show hosted by Drew Carey, which now, honestly, is kind of lame. But back in the day when a young, frisky Bob Barker was hosting, it was pretty damn awesome, which is just what your ring will be. Unlike the show, your ring will only improve with time. It's a symbol of your love for each other, and it will bring back memories of when you were two young and crazy kids in love. This will happen whether the ring is a quarter karat, half karat, or just a well-preserved carrot. Point being, you do not have to break the bank to find a ring that will be special for each of you. Figure out what is affordable for your purchase, as you would hate to be "ring poor" because you spent too much in a moment of excitement.

Does the Ring Fit?

When I ask this, I mean that the ring should fit both your finger and your lifestyle. If you do lots of hard work, lifting and hauling, or building things where your hands are always getting nicked and scratched, your ring will also get roughed up. So you probably want one to fit your lifestyle, without a lot of additional stones that could be easily dislodged. Also, make sure the thing fits your finger. Your finger will swell and shrink as you exercise or put on a few pounds because you've become fat and happy with your new life. A ring that is either too loose (easily lost) or too tight (uncomfortable) simply won't do for daily wear.

Get with the Wedding Program!

- Remember that you want to look sharp on this day of all days. If you can find room in the budget, consider buying your suit instead of just renting. Even the "experts" give the advice to spend moderately on the suit or tux and pay a good tailor.

- Speaking of your ensemble, follow the general guidelines concerning time of day and overall formality of the proceedings. There are still so many ways a groom can personalize his look, you don't have to worry about a generic look. Make sure you look just a little more formal than your groomsmen, a subtle reminder of who gets the girl today.

- Explore different variations of the attire for yourself and the groomsmen. You may also want to have a visual differentiation between the best man and the groomsmen.

- As you are picking out wedding rings, keep a few things in mind. First, make a budget and spend accordingly. Before you go out shopping, get an idea of what you want your ring to look like as far as materials and/or design. Your rings don't really have to match—it is your wedding after all—but it would be nice if there was something tying them together, such as an inscription or color. Finally, make sure your ring fits just right so it's not easily lost (too loose) or uncomfortable (too tight). You are going to be wearing it all day, every day.

CHAPTER 8

The Devil's in the F#$*ing Details

Okay, so you've probably figured out by now that you and your fiancée are planning a major undertaking. Your wedding will possibly involve a rehearsal dinner, a ceremony, and a reception. You are planning on providing food and entertainment for the guests, and each venue will have to be nicely decorated. You will need a celebrant who can perform the ceremony, a place to hold these events, and of course you will want it all documented for posterity.

Feeling overwhelmed yet?

Planning a wedding can truly be a huge undertaking depending on the size of the guest list, as well as how much lead time you give yourselves before the wedding. There are many variables in play here, but we are going to pretend you are planning your own wedding (no wedding planner) and that you are at least keeping an eye on the budget. To this end, we will attempt to give cost-saving ideas where they may apply. So in this chapter, we will try to bring up some of the little details that you may not have thought of and a few tips to help you with your gift registry and wedding providers, among other things.

As you work with the caterers mentioned in this chapter, keep in mind that you should always ask them for the contact information of past clients. Sure, they are going to cherry-pick the ones they give you, but if you speak to two or three different clients, you are sure to get a feel for how the overall event went. If all else fails, just ask them the old "What could they have done better?" It's sure to bring out something the caterer (or photographer, etc.) could work on. If you hear it more than once, then factor that into your decision.

Gift Registry

This is an exciting time, where you get to land the woman of your dreams, start a new life together, and throw a huge party for your family and friends to celebrate the whole thing. It's a lot of work, and even though you are probably too well mannered to come out and say it, you are looking forward to receiving great gifts from your guests. Enter the gift registry, where you give your guests some not-so-subtle guidance on exactly what gifts you may like to receive.

Somewhere in your mind right now, you may be flashing to a montage from a wedding movie of you and your BTB playing in the department stores, using the registry scanners like play guns as you giggle and have a blast. But a more likely scenario is her asking you if these dishes are *the* dishes you should have to start your lives together. As you look blankly back at her, she says, "These may be the dishes our children eat off of." All of a sudden, you're not thinking about dishes anymore but about how she pluralized the word *children*. See how quickly things can escalate?

Like anything wedding-related, creating your gift registry will go a little more smoothly—for both you *and* your bride-to-be—if you have a plan. Here are some tips to help you out:

Register Early

It is kind of fun actually, going to spend time with your honey and picking out things you would like others to purchase for you. It is even better if you are looking to get much-needed items for a new place to live together. Don't sweat your differences in taste. I mean, are you that fired up over what your dinner plates look like? Register early so all of those family members who want to jump on the "good" gifts will have a chance to get started. (What is a good gift? Well, I know a bad one. Who wants to give somebody a gravy boat? Boring!) Go ahead and knock this out as soon as you get a chance. You want to be able to include your registry information for interested guests.

Register for What You Need

Registering for gifts is a great way for the two of you to get your home up to par, and you should start by registering for the things that you really need. When registering, keep the following in mind:

- **Kitchen items:** Do either of you know how to cook? Or do you like to have friends over? Spruce things up with new pots, pans, silverware, dishes, etc. Even if you don't cook a lot, you will want some of the basics like dishes, silverware, and blender.
- **Be futuristic:** Planning on moving to a bigger home someday? Or having children? Buy eight place

settings instead of four. Register for that fine china you don't really want. The only thing worse than biting the bullet and registering for fine china is paying for it yourself in two years.

You can also go room by room and see what you may be lacking. Do you need new bath towels? A toaster? Maybe you are in sore need of new bedding, as hers is a spring floral pattern and yours says *Star Wars*. Remember, you may feel the urge to go for that margarita machine, but fill in the basics first.

For Your Fiancée

When it comes to the registry, you will quickly get to see if you and your fiancée are on the same page. If so, then things will go very smoothly. But if she is debating between bath towels and different types of cotton and thread counts for sheets, don't despair. It is this kind of sensible thinking that you need sometimes. So enthusiastically rub your cheek on the sample sheets and know she is making your future dwelling a comfortable place to be. ∎

Register at Several Stores

When it comes to registering, variety is key, so don't just pick a local store that has a website. Many people want to look at an item before they just ship it your way. Besides, who knows if granny is ready to surf the Internet? She may be worried about identity theft for all you know and simply will not give her credit card to any website. So select a few stores, preferably at least one that has a brick-and-mortar option for those guests who want to look before they buy. This can also be convenient for guests who live in various locations that have some stores but not others. If you pick several well-known stores with physical locations as well as online shopping options, you will be doing all you can to make it easy for them to buy you a nice gift. And there's nothing wrong with that, now is there?

High/Low

Do your best to register for gifts at various price points. Not everyone is able to buy you that multiburner, smoker-attached Weber grill you registered for. At the same time, good guests will want to bring a gift to the reception so they don't look (or feel) like total freeloaders. Please don't leave these folks only able to afford a fork from your ultra-expensive place setting for your dining room. That is why registering can be exhausting and take so much time. You have to carefully select each item, because chances are you will get many of them as gifts, so you want to be sure to find things you really need.

Straight Cash, Homey

Just like the great American "poet" and athlete Randy Moss stated, you may simply want to encourage your guests to send you money, or as Randy phrased it, "Straight cash, homey!" How do I say this? It is a very delicate subject. You don't want your guests to feel like they are being pickpocketed. Unless your large Italian family in the waste disposal business lines up to give you $100 handshakes at the receiving line, it is tough to get the word out to send money, and some guests may not like it. The worst thing you can do is put "Cash Donation Preferred" or the website of the gift registry on the wedding invitation. It's bad form. If you don't understand why, it's okay. Just don't do it. The best thing you can do is to try and let your family quietly spread the word that you are taking any donation toward the down payment on your new home. Not everyone will like this, and you will still get some blenders and salt-and-pepper shakers. Just wanted to give you a heads-up. One form of compromise on this issue is to register for gift cards at some of your favorite stores. It is still like asking for cash, but you can't take gift cards to Vegas and bet them on the "pass" line.

Be Mr. Manners

Hopefully your fiancée is well versed in wedding etiquette, but I suspect many grooms are not. Wedding etiquette says that you can include registry information on bridal shower invitations or on a separate piece of paper with the wedding invitation. There are a couple of rules you need to make sure to follow, like do not use presents that come before the wedding. If for some reason it got called off, you are supposed to return everything.

Say Thanks!

So many of your guests are going to be very generous with their gifts to you. It's the least you can do to sit down and write them a simple thank-you note. Texts and e-mails do not cut it. Please, no blind copy e-mails! "Dear Guest, Thanks for your gift." Don't let it overwhelm you; once you get going on them, you will find your rhythm.

For Your Fiancée

Along this journey, I have counseled you to take on jobs that you can execute successfully, but to not bite off more than you can chew. One such task is writing thank-you notes to guests that you know better than your bride and guests from your side of the family. It may not be the most exciting activity, but do it for your future bride. Just imagine how you would feel writing a note to her Aunt Ethel. ■

Flowers

Okay. So something tells me you will not be intimately involved in the flower selection process. But as long as we are here, let's look at a few basics that we should cover just in case you want to impress your future bride with your knowledge of the floral selection process.

The Reason for the Season

Remember, there really are no bad ideas when it comes to selecting flowers for the ceremony and reception. It brings a touch of nature and class to the proceedings. There are, however, more and less expensive choices depending on the time of year. I thought that might get your attention! So try to stay within the choices (or guide your bride to stay within the choices) that are in season for your wedding. This will prevent you from having to dedicate such a large portion of the budget to flowers. Do you want to drop some knowledge on her? Let her know that orchids, roses, and tulips are beautiful year-round flowers she may want to consider. Iris and pansies? That's so winter seasonal!

Budget

Set a cost for the floral decor at your wedding and reception and stick to it. If cost versus quality of flower becomes an issue, really think about where flowers will have the most impact. For example, the bride should hold a beautiful bouquet if that's her dream, but there may not need to be fresh arrangements on every table at the reception. If you are looking for more options to stretch your budget, faux flowers are an option, as they look closer to the real thing than they used to. Some have even taken to growing their own flowers to save money. This requires true dedication, I know, but maybe it's something your green-thumbed mother-in-law can help with?

Money can't buy you happiness, so you might as well give it to us.
—Dave Barry, columnist, on the motto of the wedding industry

Photography and Video

Guys, whether you like it or not, wedding photos are important. When you are an old and gray-haired codger, you will want great photo (and video) memories of your wedding to look back on and remember the day. You will need them because at this point your mind will have failed you! If you have children later down the road, they will want to know about the wedding, and a picture really is worth a thousand words. Since both you and your bride will need to be in the pictures and since these pictures need to be done right, most couples bring in a professional to do the job. Here are some criteria you should follow when selecting a photographer/videographer:

Search and Destroy
You will need to get cracking on finding your photographer as soon as your proposal has been accepted. You may have noticed that there are certain times of the year when most people prefer to get married, and you are no exception. The best photographers will book up fast, so you will want to get out there, find someone you want to work with, and get him or her booked. Otherwise you will be stuck with Aunt Ethel and her Polaroid camera.

I Know a Guy

Ask around to anyone you know who recently got married. Peruse their album and see if you like the photographer's style. You will also find good photographers by asking the other vendors you may be interacting with, such as the wedding planner, cake artist, caterer, florist, etc. Wedding professionals make up a little community, and they know who does good work (and who doesn't). Many of the best wedding photographers also offer video packages. If you feel a great level of comfort with their professionalism and ability, you may have them handle both.

Look at Samples

Once you start narrowing down the choices, you will want to do a lot of viewing of the photographers' sample work. You can begin to rule out providers based on their price and style. If your wedding is outdoors, see if they have any examples of outdoor wedding photos. Hopefully most who do this for a living can pull off a simple "bride and groom" shot, so see how they use their creativity. Look at the angles or close-ups they use, and how they arrange guests. On the video side, it is all about getting the guests to give memorable messages and well wishes to you. Ask if they do anything unique or prompt the guests with a funny or interesting question to get them talking.

Meet and Greet

You cannot be traipsing all over town, meeting with every photographer in the phone book. Even if you could, why would you want to? Narrow the field down to about three different vendors, and then do some face-to-face meetings. Do they seem professional? Do they have a good personality that could bring out the best in your photos? If you have children that will be an integral part of the wedding, have they worked extensively with kids? Most photographers will have additional albums available for you to look at. Try to go through an entire recent wedding album. It will give you an idea of what to expect.

Here are some questions you should ask the photographer and videographer:

- Is my wedding date available? (seems like a good place to start!)
- How long have you been doing this?
- Have you worked a wedding this size and style before?
- How would you describe your style (both photography and videography)? If they can't define it, it's probably not a good sign.
- May I have a list of references?

Also, throw them a curveball to see how they react. If you say, "Hey, we are considering a zoo-themed wedding with guests dressed like zoo animals," do they smile and get excited or crinkle their nose with snobbery? You can get a feel for them that way. You don't have to be best friends with your photographer or videographer, but you don't want the people documenting your event to think the premise of your event is beneath them either.

Negotiate

If you haven't learned this yet, there is usually room for negotiation with service professionals. Unless they are simply far and away the best, or it is just in their DNA not to do it, most will be able to offer something extra if you ask. You may be able to negotiate just the price, or you may be able to add a few additional extras to your package, like a free album or additional prints. The catch is that if you don't ask, they will not ask you if you want more for the same price. There should be a contract that you sign to make everything official. No matter how nice they are, make sure everything you've agreed to is clearly stated in the contract. If it is not in there, then that vendor is not responsible for providing it to you.

Food and Drinks

Eat, drink, and be merry! A feast of plenty is part of the wedding experience, and for many, an open bar is part of the fun as well. Food and drink are an integral part of the wedding experience for your guests, and you want them to enjoy themselves. And nothing leaves an impression on your attendees like good food—or food that's gone horribly wrong. Now, you are not running a theme park, but you also do not want a bunch of your family feeling sick because you decided to serve some "day-old" food you found on the cheap. So let's see how to navigate the first part of "Eat, drink, and be merry" for your guests.

Catering

First off, you will need a caterer. If there is one that is part of your wedding venue, then you may end up picking them as part of a package deal, but even if this is the case, you will want to brainstorm a few ideas of your own for the type of food you are considering. Ask yourselves if you are going to do "heavy hors d'oeuvres," a buffet, or a sit-down dinner with a set menu. Not all caterers can execute all styles, so make sure your vision fits with something the caterer has done before. You will of course need to make this fit with the time of year, venue, and theme or level of formality of the rest of your plans. There is one last consideration, and instead of hitting you over the head with it, I will give you a hint: It rhymes with "wudget." How many expected guests multiplied by caterer cost per guest (per plate, as you will hear) equals, drumroll please, your estimated food cost! As long as you are sticking to your total cost allocation, let's look at other factors you will want to use to select your caterer:

What Type of Food Do You Want?

Does your caterer specialize in only certain types of foods? It is a tricky balance finding the right caterer who isn't too specialized, yet is able to provide excellent food with a lot of options for you to select from. It is always nice to match the menu to the theme or location of your wedding. You can serve seafood at a beach wedding, etc. You may also choose to serve a type of food that's special for your relationship or culture. Have a large Italian family? Maybe you want to serve Italian food. Was your first date at a French bistro? Maybe French food should be served. As always, ask your guests if they have any special dietary considerations you need to account for.

Keep It Unique

If you have an old family recipe for an old family favorite, something that reminds you of special times with your family, see if the caterer is open to preparing it for your reception. I mean, it's cool and all to have a carving station for roast beef, but is that something unique to the two of you? If possible, make it beforehand yourself with the help of family and give the caterer simple, final instructions. It's just a nice personal touch to share something special in your life with your guests.

Taste Test

If you are considering using a specific caterer for your wedding, set up an appointment to sample the goods. Ask how many people they will be okay with you bringing to the tasting. You will want a few family members and/or friends there to get their feedback as well. Opinions on food can vary, and if you happen to love a caterer's, you want to make sure it appeals to many, not just to your specific tastes.

What's in It for Me?

When you hear a caterer quote a price, do a little digging. What exactly does that price include? Will the caterer provide tables and chairs? Do you even need tables and chairs? Will the person you are meeting with be there to act as a coordinator, or will it be a bunch of uninterested hired hands? You will want to ask a lot of detailed questions to see what exactly the caterer will do and will not do (such as provide and serve alcohol) and a written agreement what will and will not be provided. You want to find out exactly what you'll get for your money before you sign on the dotted line.

License and Registration, Please

Is the caterer licensed? This is usually an indication of a quality operation. Ask if they provide alcohol (if you are having a bar), and if they do, make sure they have their permit. Ask if they only use a set wine list, or if you can customize. Basically you are looking for any way you can to have as many options as possible. If you are using the same caterer for food and bar service, don't forget to ask for a discount on the total. You can ask them to separate their price and compare their bar service price to other providers.

Setting the Table

Ask if you can see photos or examples of past setups, especially if you are asking for different stations or different tables placed around a reception room. You will want to make sure you have the right team to match the decisions you have in place for your event. For example, you do not want a caterer who specializes in children's birthday parties to be your reception caterer, no matter how good the chicken fingers are.

For Your Fiancée

A florist? A baker? Can I get a discount on the music maker? Yes, if you are having the "big" wedding complete with dinner, dancing, and drinks for all, then it will seem like something you could possibly put on your resume. You will be skilled in the art of negotiation, learn to manage (and scream at) others, and drive to the final goal of throwing one big party/celebration to mark the beginning of your life-long marital bliss. If your fiancée isn't comfortable with the negotiation part of the transaction, then take this off her plate. You like to get in there and get a good deal, so use your talents here. Also, recognize your strengths and weaknesses as a couple. If she negotiates mergers and acquisitions for a living, go sit in the car. ■

Wedding Cake

Ah, one of the most time-honored traditions: the wedding cake. It just doesn't seem to be a wedding without a beautiful cake. But who should bake it? And what should it look like? A great cake isn't just tasty; it is also visually stunning. A memorable cake will be something that does more than feed the guests something sweet after dinner; it will be more of a "conversation piece" and will almost act as part of the decor. And trust me when I tell you that, as uninvolved as you were (or wish you were!) with some of the other areas of the wedding planning, this is one part you will want to be front and center for. After all, who doesn't want to go to a great bakery and sample cake? So here's some info on how to get the best wedding cake ever . . .

Nuptial Knowledge

True or False: Feeding wedding cake to your spouse is just a nice photo opportunity.

■ False. It is based on the tradition (of ancient Rome, Japa-nese couples, and Jewish couples, among others) of sharing food for good luck. This idea is an offshoot of the "sharing the first piece of wedding cake" tradition, which is supposed to form a bond between the husband and wife.

Save the Date

If you are trying to book a very popular cake designer, you will have to meet with him or her months in advance to get on his or her schedule. This isn't something you want to fiddle around with, as the cake will make a guest appearance in most wedding photo albums and be captured, for better or for worse, in all of its timeless beauty (hopefully).

Easy-Bake

Making the cake taste good isn't the primary challenge for your cake artist (I hope). The challenge is making a dream cake that fits in with the two of you and your wedding. Maybe your bride has determined that, for your beach-themed wedding, the cake should be covered in frosting that looks like seashells or your BTB immortalized as a scantily clad mermaid made of frosting. Now we're talking! (Just kidding). If you do not have a specific cake in mind, share with the prospective chef pieces from your wedding, a picture of your bride's wedding dress (if you can get your bride-to-be to let you see it), or anything you can bring to give a sense of your wedding's personality. See what the chef comes up with, what inspiration he or she takes from what you shared. You may be looking for a cake similar to one he or she has done before, only with a few adjustments. Or maybe you will inspire that chef in a whole new direction!

A Taste Sensation

Even though taste isn't the main thing people will remember about your wedding cake, it's still pretty important. Once you think you have your cake artist narrowed down to two or three choices, set up a tasting. Call ahead and let them know which flavors you would like to sample, and you and your BTB can maybe bring a friend (or two). Some bakeries with sterling reputations no longer do tastings, but those are usually the ones that are the most reputable. If you insist on tasting samples, then you will have to find a bakery that will accommodate your desire for a preview. You can always ask them if you can purchase something that would help you decide, like cupcakes in the flavors you're interested in.

Holy Sheet

If you are having a really sizable wedding, then the cost you'll spend on your cake can add up real fast. If you've found that you'll need to order a ten-layer monstrosity in order to feed all of your guests, you will want to know this trick. You likely don't want to pay your cake designer to make a customized cake to feed 100 guests, so what is generally done is this: You design and size a cake to fit your budget, and then have sheet cakes made in the same cake and frosting style as the original. Have it all cut behind the scenes, and nobody is the wiser.

Photo Opportunity

Make sure your photographer has scheduled some shots of you with the cakes. Consult with your photographer on different angles, sightlines, surrounding yourselves with flowers, etc. That way you can be assured you are getting some nice pictures. You can do the classic "join hands and cut" plus the always fun "cake smear" on each other's faces. Decide beforehand when you are going to do this—you'll want to cut the cake either right after the reception starts or with an hour or two to go. Aunt Ethel doesn't want to miss the cake, but she doesn't want to stay out all night to wait for it, either. As for what exactly you do once you are up there, there really isn't a protocol. You may want to plan something out with your bride, or hey, just wing it!

For Your Fiancée

When you see your bride on the wedding day, you will notice how ravishing she looks. You may notice how her entire ensemble works together, and there is a reason for that. It is because she spent months planning for this day. In addition to her natural beauty, she had her hair styled, selected just the right makeup, and paid a pretty penny for it all, too. So you may want to ask beforehand if it's okay to smear a bunch of cake on her. People came for a wedding, not to see your funeral. ■

Doom and Groom

Don't worry guys, you are not doomed. The men's lobby has worked hard to get you just a little slice of individuality on the cake issue. Enter the groom's cake. Basically, the groom's cake is your chance to show a little bit of your own personality during the wedding ceremony. A quick scan of Pinterest will show groom's cakes from an alma mater (Go Stetson!), to a Homer Simpson cake, to a cake shaped like a bottle of Tabasco sauce. Everything from Bud Light to Batman makes an appearance, a clear sign that you should have free reign on this (and only this) issue. Have your ideas at hand and make sure the cake specialist is on board with your vision, however strange it may be. Your BTB may want your input, but in many cases she will get your cake done as a surprise for you, and you won't know exactly what you are getting until it is brought in at the reception.

For Your Fiancée

At times, you and your bride may begin to feel overwhelmed by the enormity of planning your wedding, reception, and rehearsal dinner. Take a quick break and have dinner together, or watch a movie. Take your mind off the wedding for just a few hours. Then the two of you will be ready to dive back in. ■

Music

Music plays an integral part in weddings, and depending on your church (if you are getting married in a church) and your venue, you will want music for both the ceremony and the reception. Maybe I should say that you will need to hire two musicians, because the band that can rock out your reception and make people dance may not be the best choice to play music as your BTB walks down the aisle. So keep that in mind as we move forward in this chapter: separate but equal music providers, as well as some other thoughts on how to prepare to make beautiful music together as a married couple.

Ceremony Music

Music is very important for the wedding ceremony. You want your guests to enjoy the music, and the music helps them celebrate your wedding. Fortunately, there are timeless and preapproved songs that belong at your wedding ceremony, which means that hiring a skilled wedding musician should not be too hard. Many people hire the musicians and/or choir of their church of choice. You can discuss this with the pastor or the representative with whom you are making the arrangements.

Reception Music

The ceremony is the reason you and your family and friends are gathered here today. But once you have tied the knot, it is on to the reception. The music at your reception is almost as important as the food and decor. It touches every guest and definitely sets the mood. Let's get into the decision . . .

Band or DJ?

Band or DJ? This is a timeless question. How do you choose? Well, much of the decision will be dictated by your other decisions. Is the feel of your wedding casual or formal? What is the setting? A DJ will have the ability to pull from many different genres, styles, and generations of music. You can give them playlists, etc. A live band can be riskier, because selecting a band requires a bit of a guess, and you can only hope they sound as good as they did when you went to their live show and drank a few beers. A band will also be limited by which songs they know how to play. Don't discount splitting the evening between some classy dinner music from your iPod with a band to bring it home! This can save a few bucks, as most bands do a package for a certain amount of hours. But you may not need the band for the speeches and dinner, hence the iPod solution.

Taste Test

Here is the other music issue at hand: Not everyone likes the music that you happen to like. We know Grandma Maude and Uncle Joe don't know who today's bands are, so try to make sure there is something there for everyone. These are your guests at your wedding so you would like them to have fun. Besides, what could be more fun for you than to see some of your older family members turn back the clock for a few minutes and show off their moves? Get a good feel for the band and what songs they play. Do they play songs from all different eras? Do they know countless covers of popular songs, past and present? Make sure they are a good fit for what you want.

Master of Ceremonies

If you have a DJ, he or she can often double as the master of ceremonies, especially if the person works a lot of weddings. Talk to him or her to see if they are willing (and able) to perform these duties. You will want to make sure the DJ is willing to guide you from his or her experience and make suggestions, but not simply play the music he or she likes.

Nuptial Knowledge

What is the most popular song at weddings?

■ No, it's not "YMCA." We are talking about the wedding, not the reception. The real answer is Pachelbel's Canon in D.

Transportation

This one seems easy, right? Call a limo service, and book it. Well, there are a few quick things I would do to make sure things go smoothly. You will want to plan out where you want them to take you. For example, do you and your wedding party need a lift from the church to the reception? Do you and your bride want a lift from the reception to the hotel, airport, etc.? Get the logistics down, and then make sure the limo company can accommodate. If you are planning on having a shuttle for guests back to the hotel (always a good idea), then see if you can find one company that can do it all for you. They will be more invested to take good care of everyone. Even if everything looks A-okay with them, don't forget to . . .

- **Ask for References:** Ask for references from wedding-related vendors as to which limo services are reputable. There would be nothing worse than to be without transportation from the church to the reception.
- **Bring Refreshments:** If you are so inclined, place someone from the wedding party in charge of packing a cooler for the ride.
- **Make Memories:** Assign someone else to bring a point-and-shoot camera into the limo. I know lots of couples who had the best time on their limo ride. You may want a few shots to document it.

Whatever your ride, make sure you have fun on your ride to the church or to the reception. You know what people relate as one of the best ideas they have had? Have the limo make an unscheduled stop on the way to the reception. Maybe a dive bar, or a place with killer desserts. As long as you have the time to kill, do something fun and unscheduled to break the tension of the big day and for a fun memory for you and the wedding party.

Premarital Counseling

You have decided to tie the knot, to get hitched, to take the plunge, or even to jump the broom. And now that you've decided to spend the rest of your life with your bride-to-be, you want to make sure that you have years of happiness ahead of you, which means that now is the time to talk about some of the tough stuff that you may not have brought up before. After all, most couples that are headed to the altar do not often randomly blurt out, "How much should we save for retirement? Do you think Social Security will be there at all for us?" Sometimes they do not express other important views on issues like how many children each believes is the "right" number, or even if they think they want children at all. These issues and more can be broached with some guidance, and you will soon be able to tell where the areas of concern are or, to put it plainly, what you guys will fight about. Enter premarital counseling.

Premarital counseling is a type of therapy done through your church or with a marriage and family therapist that helps couples prepare for their life of marital bliss. Depending on your religious affiliation, your church may require you and your BTB to go through your church's marriage counseling encounter before you can be married in that specific faith. Basically, without all of the counseling speak, you hire a professional to help the two of you figure out what issues may arise in your lives together, whether that be physical, mental, financial, or sexual. It usually consists of five to seven sessions where you discuss serious life issues, but there are some programs that just fit everything into a single weekend. Each of you is usually given a written list of questions to fill out, without knowing the other person's responses. I am not really speaking of cosmetic things like "Do you want carpet or hardwood in our house?" but more along the lines of the following:

- Do you want to have children? Ideally, when do you see that occurring?
- Financially, what are your goals, and how do you like to spend any discretionary income?
- Do you like to live within a planned budget?
- Do you see us having joint or separate accounts?
- Let's talk about sex (baby). Are you okay discussing your preferences?
- How important is faith to you on a day-to-day basis?
- How do you see mundane things (like household chores) being divided?
- Do you see vacations as frivolous or important?
- Are there any traits about your fiancé(e) that really bother you?
- Is there anything in your past that may come up at a later date?
- Do you have any previous marriages or children that you have never discussed?
- Do you have massive debt or student loans?

Maybe you think a man should never clean the house or cook a meal. Maybe she thinks a woman shouldn't have to work. Maybe you think children should be spanked and she doesn't. I know, this sounds like as much fun as a barrel of monkeys. When they ask you questions like "What don't you like about your fiancée?" you may feel like you need to break out your best Admiral Ackbar impression ("It's a trap!"). But these questions are structured to make you two think and see where the difference of opinions may be before you get married. Hopefully you can find enough common ground on these things so that the two of you can live together happily ever after. Also, if you have major differences of opinion on some of these matters, it is important to know that ahead of time. You will also notice an inordinate amount of questions concerning money and sex. These are the top two reasons couples split up, so you may as well cover them now.

Nuptial Knowledge

What percentage of adults aged eighteen to twenty-nine are married?

■ Just 20 percent of adults aged 18–29 are married. The trend is moving toward getting married later in life and, as a result, starting families later in life as well. But maybe this works out, as the average life expectancy is increasing as well.

Get with the Wedding Program!

- When you are planning an event this big, the details matter. Doing the hard work ahead of time to coordinate the caterer, photographer, etc., will all pay dividends when your big day comes. Your wedding day will be hectic enough without suddenly needing a ride from the church to the ceremony because the limo didn't show up!

- Creating your gift registry will give your wedding guests some guidance on what you would like to receive as a wedding gift. Remember, the keys are to register early, register at more than one store, and register for a wide price range of gifts. This will allow guests several ways to find something for you.

- Remember not to open the gifts that arrive before your wedding date. On the other side, get your thank-you notes out quickly.

- You may not be really selective about the floral decor at your event, but your bride may be. Make sure you budget accordingly.

- It is really fun to have photo and video keepsakes of your wedding and reception. Who wouldn't want to remember Uncle Alan on the dance floor? Ask around to couples you may know who recently got married or somebody in one of the wedding-related businesses that you have already selected. All of the professionals in the area know who does a great job.

- At your wedding, you will probably be feeding your guests in some way, shape, or form. So whether it's a buffet-style dinner, heavy hors d'oeuvres, or just cocktail weenies, you should consider hiring a caterer if your wedding budget can stand it. It will take a lot of work off of your and your family's plate and allow for a more enjoyable event.

- Another important item to consider hiring a professional for is the wedding cake. As you may have seen on TV, they can do quite creative things with cakes! Oh, and don't forget the groom's cake. It is a chance for you to really express something about yourself, or have a man's cake.

- As far as entertaining your guests, you will want some music at the reception to help set the mood. Smooth jazz for cocktail hour, or classic R&B when it's time to dance, your music selections touch every guest in attendance. Provide a wide array of songs, so every guest has a chance to dance, even the older ones who refer to it as "cutting a rug."

- Line up reliable transportation for yourselves from the church to reception, reception to airport, or wherever you are headed. Make sure if you are including the wedding party in the ride to the reception, the limo company has a vehicle to hold everyone. It's okay to use the less formal "limo coach," as the main thing is to bring all of you together for a few minutes to celebrate your (very) recent marriage.

- It is strongly advisable to attend some form of premarital counseling session. Let's face it, you probably wouldn't have these tough conversations with each other without this type of forum. It will help you identify what areas the two of you disagree on and in which areas you are of a single mind.

CHAPTER 9

Events Before—and After— the Big Event

Your wedding is the part of this entire thing that has the most meaning. You are declaring your love for each other, and are willing to legally marry one another in the bonds of holy matrimony. It has ramifications as far as health benefits, the rights of your children, and on down the line. But there are also all of the events surrounding the actual ceremony that are further celebration of the event. We are going to focus on these events in this chapter. If I happen to describe the bachelor party with particular zeal and fervor, hey, please don't judge.

Bachelor Party

First, please know that each bachelor party is beautiful in its own way. It's a rite of passage to have a bachelor party, one last symbolic "guy's night" when a wedding is in the near future. If you are thinking to yourself that all bachelor parties are an excuse to act foolish, drink too much, and re-enact the "good old days" with your friends, then you would be right—and wrong. You can define what you want your celebration to be about.

For the most part, today's men have realized that marriage should be celebrated, and grooms do not need to be sent off to marriage with some sort of celebration of debauchery like you're heading off to a battle from which you may never return. Hopefully for all concerned you are excited about entering into this union and shouldn't treat it as if you are almost certainly facing death.

Read it and weep fellas . . . UNO!

—From Smosh.com's article,

"20 Signs of the Worst Bachelor Party Ever"

So now that my sermon is complete, we can continue. When you take away strip clubs and their ilk, you and your groomsmen still want to do something fun. So do not shy away from the bachelor party because you think the way others behave is outlandish. Instead, try to think of something everyone can enjoy that would be a "special event," something you will all remember. Some ideas that may work, depending on your geography, include:

- **Vegas:** We will just put it here and get it over with. I will not go into great detail here, as those who are headed to Las Vegas will know what to do. Remember, keep it legal.
- **Poker Tourney:** I think this is a pretty underrated option. Think about it: cards, betting, bragging

rights, steaks, and beer. If you can incorporate it around a huge sporting event to have on in the background, then all the better. There will be a group that is in for all day and all night, but it will allow others to come by for a few hours if that's all they can spare. The whole thing will cost about the same as a plane ticket or two, at the most.

- **Golf:** If you have a group of hackers who like to go out and tear up the fairway (or rough), then plan a weekend golf trip. Dads and fathers-in-law can get in on this if you so choose. You can pick a place near a beach, or rent a lake house if you can somehow get your hands on a ski boat. Then you can golf in the morning and have some downtime on the boat or on the beach.

- **Paintball:** Nothing gets the competitive juices flowing like a little competition where you are trying to "kill" each other.

- **Go Fish:** This can be of the freshwater, fly, or even the deep-sea variety. This is a good group trip because, unlike golf, it is something everyone can get involved in, even if they have no prior experience.

- **Hey, Sport:** Go ahead and get tickets to a sporting event or concert that you usually wouldn't splurge for. This is a great way for the guys to have a great time together that is one of a kind.

- **Get Out of Town:** If you have a fatter budget or a friend who works for an airline, visit a new city and explore what it has to offer. Have a long lost (but really great) friend nobody gets to see? Take the party to him. Nothing beats a special surprise guest to up the ante of the trip. If you decide to leave town, just realize this may be a deal breaker for some people, so you may lose a few attendees.

- **Skeet Shoot:** Skeet shooting is a really fun activity that has that uniqueness to it. Plus, it does not require the same full-on commitment as hunting, but firearms are still involved. It never hurts to attempt to find an activity that allows more people to participate.

- **Just Hangin':** If your bachelor party is going to be more about close friends and family, try this on for size. Try to get everyone to bring some pictures of things you have done together, and/or have the elder statesmen of the group bring some of their best marriage and child-raising tips. Put it all together in an album for you to look back on. Yes, I am slightly uncomfortable with how close this is to men's scrapbooking. But it's still a cool idea. You could even do this as the first step in a long weekend of guys' activities.

You get the idea. You want something manly, but something where there will most likely not be police involvement. As for my recommendation, I like to really push the schedule, so if you put me in charge, I would probably throw you on a plane to a city where we could golf, skeet shoot, chill on the beach, and there would be a major concert or sporting event taking place. I am all in favor of ordering multiple items off that menu. But that may not be your style. Stretch yourself a little, but build in enough activities you'll for sure enjoy so that there is no chance the weekend will go off the rails. And like I said, you will have to get with your best man and make the bachelor party yours. Lots of these weekends are done as a surprise to the groom. That's fine; just be really clear with him about what is and what isn't acceptable.

Nuptial Knowledge

How was the bachelor celebrated in the '40s and '50s?

■ Back in the day, they used to have something simply called the "gentleman's dinner," where the FOG (Remember him? Father of the groom [backward]) No more hints going forward? a formal dinner where there were many toasts to the groom . . . many, many toasts. You may not have to attend a formal dinner anymore (there'll be plenty of those coming up anyway), but you can still count on at least one groomsman or stray attendee to imbibe a little too much. Just have transportation arranged beforehand and the worst that can happen will be some headaches the next day.

Bachelorette Party

This probably isn't an area that you will spend a lot of time on. Just know that long gone are the days of ladies gathering to have tea and talk about where they get their hair done. Women are up for a great time just like anybody else, so she may be going on an overnight trip with her friends or something akin to what you are doing. You have a chance at a surprise role reversal if you approach her about the rules of engagement for the weekend. It could be a good move, as it's showing that you are thinking responsibly and want to make sure nothing gets out of hand for either one of you. My only experience is when we were attacked by a bachelorette party with a bride-to-be on a "scavenger hunt." It wasn't too out of line, but they weren't collecting donations for the local church.

Bridal Shower

Oddly enough, the bridal shower is held in honor of someone who is not yet a bride (your BTB), and the showering hopefully only occurs before the event. So what exactly is this? It is a gift-giving party for the BTB thrown by her friends and family. Sometimes they go to a fancy lunch or tea room as part of it. Then they shower each other with fake laughter and backhanded compliments. You may not have a big part in this, but if it's held at a house, see if you can help set up, clean up, bring the gifts home, etc.

Jack and Jill Wedding Shower

There is a growing trend starting up that is called a "Jack and Jill" wedding shower. This is basically where the wedding shower, formally known as the bridal shower, turns co-ed. You, as a couple, invite friends and family to celebrate the pending nuptials as a group, versus your BTB and her gang of friends, as well as both of your mothers. Involving the guys (this means you!) will let the two of you have another joint event to celebrate the wedding versus the traditional girls-only affair. As a side benefit, this setup can help diffuse any tensions that may be brewing between any of the families, as the co-ed version of this gathering tends to be more casual with less drama.

Rehearsal Dinner

The rehearsal dinner is a traditional part of the wedding festivities. Its specific purpose is to get the two families together and let them get to know each other. As we discussed in Chapter 3, the groom's family usually pays for the dinner. It is often held the night before the wedding after the ceremony rehearsal, but depending on logistics and if you are hosting your wedding during a three-day weekend, you are not bound by that. Usually you would invite:

- Your immediate family (including siblings with their plus-ones)
- Your bride-to-be's immediate family (including siblings with their plus-ones)
- The wedding party
- The officiant

In addition, if the budget for the dinner is generous enough, you can even invite guests that came in from out of town so you get to spend a few extra minutes with them and so they have something to do while in town.

Venue?

Where oh where to hold the rehearsal dinner? Well, it really depends on how many people you plan to have attend. So make sure the place you are thinking of can set aside the space for the crowd you have planned. You can make this soiree happen just about anywhere, from a place as simple as the ballroom at the hotel where everyone is staying to somebody's house where you can have a cookout and play a little corn hole. Just do your guests a favor and give them a little direction as to how to dress for the event and the general theme. At a wedding I attended in Blakely, Georgia, we were invited to an event at "Uncle Bubba's" house. We expected vulture-sized mosquitos and roadkill on the barbecue. As we pulled up the driveway of a palatial estate, we quickly realized we had miscalculated and beat it back to the hotel to dress up another level or two. Don't leave your guests in the same spot.

What Takes Place?

There are a few traditional activities that take place at the rehearsal dinner. Feel free to do the rehearsal dinner your way, but there is a reason that it happens this way: You and your bride are about to get sucked into the wedding vortex. So consider knocking out the following:

- **And This Is?:** This is sometimes the first chance for the families and siblings on each side to meet each other. Unfortunately for you, it is in your best interest not to be bellied up to the bar or catching up with buddies. Rather, you should spend some time introducing everyone to each other and making sure things go smoothly.
- **For Me?:** This is a good time to give the wedding party their gifts. It should be done subtly, without a lot of fanfare so as to not make others feel left out.
- **Whole Wheat Toast:** This is usually your dad's place to do a toast. Your family gets dibs on first toast, especially if they're paying for the rehearsal dinner. After Dad's toast, you're up next, if you so choose. If you are stuck on a toast, it always pays dividends to flatter your bride and both families.

- **Choose One or the Other:** Today, couples are getting in on the act. See if your BTB wants to say a few words and welcome guests, or if she would rather you do it.

The rehearsal dinner is usually a fun, pretty low-key night for you. You will be surrounded by friends, family, and your bride's family (who is soon to be yours). That said, just so you know, there may be some sort of drama when your two families meet. I've seen the father of the groom take first toast at the rehearsal dinner when it was the father of the bride's show (meaning he paid for it). I've seen a sister of the groom tell off the father of the bride and, well . . . you get the idea. Experiences like these are what lead me to suggest that you stay on patrol for a good part of this event in an attempt to head off any problems between the families when possible. Hopefully the riot police will not be needed at your rehearsal dinner and you can just enjoy the event and get ready for the wedding.

After Party

After all of the hype, hoopla, stress, and media coverage of your wedding (well, you did hire a photographer), many couples find they are ready to just relax and have some fun. Some couples want to spend time with just each other, but others want to kick back and party. So for night owls and those who have an afternoon wedding, the "after party" was created.

It's pretty simple really. Instead of everyone asking each other, "Hey, are you going out after this?" a plan is formulated. That way you can even send out invitations to the thing if you would like to! A few cool and fun ideas include:

- **Rock and Bowl:** Nothing says fun like a bunch of dressed-up wedding-goers strapping the Velcro on their shoes and hitting the lanes. It is a fun and goofy way to blow off steam after the wedding. If you can find a location with fun music and disco lights, all the better.
- **Karaoke:** Chances are, most of the guests have had a sip or two of wine, beer, or champagne. If you are so inclined, you may want to do so as well. Getting the group together at a local karaoke bar is a great way to do something that is just plain fun. Who doesn't want to hear you belt out "My Girl"?
- **House Party:** You can go to a nearby house of a family member or relative, or even take the party up to your hotel suite if you don't have a huge group. Stock the tub with ice and mixers and tell everyone to raid their minibars.
- **Rat Pack:** If you have the budget, you could schedule a casino night with a few small prizes for most play chips won. Hold a poker game with an open bar in the hotel ballroom. Having an organized activity where everyone can mingle and have fun is the main point. Since there are casinos popping up all over the place, you could even road trip there for the night.

A few points of interest: You may be running out of budget at this point in the planning process, so you may just want to get a local pub to section off some tables for you and your group. Also, if your group is a group that enjoys drinking, you should find a way to provide transportation for these folks. At this point you will not be trying to show up in a fleet of limos. Limo companies often have a variety of vehicles, and sometimes you can get them to cut you a deal on having a large van for this type of thing. Get a few responsible types (read: your best man) to help assure that no guest is left behind. Also, you may want to plan an after party for your guests, but you may be a no-show. You and your bride may have other ideas on your mind, and everyone will understand if you want to start spending time together, like, right now.

Morning-After Brunch

If your wedding was held in the evening, the reception may have gone late enough that no more partying was required. If your budget is there, then it can be nice to have a send-off brunch the next morning, especially for the out-of-town guests. If you and your bride aren't on an airplane, it is always nice to have a post–ceremony and reception "debrief" session with all of your guests. It is especially a nice thing to do for those guests that traveled long distances to bear witness to your ceremony (and drink your booze). The easiest thing to do is to have this event at the hotel where guests are staying. I modestly suggest you do it at a restaurant if possible, even having locals pick up out-of-town guests from the hotel.

Honeymoon

The honeymoon is a wedding tradition all couples look forward to. After the wedding reception—and maybe the "after party" or morning-after brunch—most couples try to plan some form of vacation together. After all, what better way for the two of you to start your lives together than with a memorable vacation?

Of course, if the world is your oyster and your budget hasn't been devastated by the wedding, then planning this trip just became much easier. What you need to do is pick several possibilities, like a week of skiing, or possibly a trip to visit Mickey Mouse. Maybe a tropical cruise, or wine tasting in California? Get your list together and jot down the pros and cons of each. You should begin this planning in conjunction with your wedding planning so you can make sure your budget can handle the honeymoon that you want.

For Your Fiancée

We've talked about being committed, and we mean it. Try to find a few ways to make the honeymoon extra special for your new bride. Her favorite flowers could decorate your room, or have a case of her favorite sparkling water (or wine) on hand. Little touches that show you know her and appreciate her. Besides, it's likely she carried more of the wedding planning burden, so it's a way to say "Thanks." ∎

Once you have narrowed your field, look at trip length and cost. How much time can you get off from work? How long can you afford to stay? Although begging guests for money is considered poor form, it is okay for your families to put the word out amongst each other that you are in need of some funds for your honeymoon. It may be a fine line, but instead of a money grab, you are seeking cash to help fund a wedding-related event.

Now there are even resorts and destinations that will let you register for things you want to include in your honeymoon that wedding well-wishers can purchase as a wedding gift. If you are all about the honeymoon experience, this may be something to consider.

Where you may travel will be dependent on what your interests are and what time of year you will be traveling. Here are a few tips, tricks, and recommendations to take into consideration when you make your list:

- **Clocks:** Time is of the essence. If you only have a three- or five-day trip planned, make sure you won't be spending too much of it en route. Traveling to some destination without a nearby airport, say Lake Tahoe, requires a flight plus a drive, which will eat into your time to chill-lax.
- **Be Extreme:** Or don't. Just make sure if you have planned a bungee jump and zipline excursion, your spouse is on the same page. She may have booked all-day massages and spa treatments. This should be time you spend together, not on separate vacations while sharing a hotel room.
- **Consider This:** You may want to do a few quick trip estimates, and then turn the planning over to a travel agent. Give them as many specifics as possible. This will save you a lot of time and effort running down hotel deals, multiple flight scenarios for multiple airlines, rent-a-car, etc. You may be kind of busy planning your wedding after all.
- **It Makes the World Go 'Round:** Well, let's all hope the answer to what makes the world go around is love, but I suspect money is in the top two on the list. Despite all of the "deals" out there, the bottom line is that you usually get what you pay for when

you travel. Make sure your room is of good comfort and quality. You don't want to be roughing it on your honeymoon, unless you decide to go camping.

There you have it. Your honeymoon plans should reflect things you like to do as a couple, with a destination that is as exciting as it is affordable to you. Put your heads together and figure out what will be the best course when you take into consideration things like vacation from work, etc. In the front of your mind should be that the two of you are together, so hopefully you can have a good time just about anywhere. The honeymoon will be an exciting start to your lives together, a little bit of time for the two of you to just enjoy a vacation together as newlyweds.

Nuptial Knowledge

What is the origin of the word *honeymoon*?

■ *Honeymoon* is derived from an ancient European custom where the newly married bride and groom drank honey beer for a month, or lunar cycle. Hence the phrasing *honey*, for the honey mead, and *moon*, for the month or lunar cycle. Another interpretation, related more to the tradition of taking a secluded trip and not the name, is drawn from the Norse tradition of stealing a bride from a neighboring tribe, and then hiding until the bride's tribe gave up the search. I guess if you combine these two interpretations, you get to today, where we go off to an all-inclusive resort in the tropics and drink all we can for a week or so.

Get with the Wedding Program!

- The wedding ceremony is the all-important reason for the gathering of all of your (and your bride's) friends and family. The "dearly beloved," if you will. Don't lose sight of that! But along with the wedding comes a slate of events that occur both before and after you tie the knot. So in addition to the ceremony, the traditional wedding will include events like the bachelor (and bachelorette) party, the rehearsal dinner, the reception, and the honeymoon, among others.

- The bachelor party is a rite of passage for soon-to-be grooms. It is a symbolic last night for the guys to be together. This can truly be a "party," or it can take whatever shape and form that you want it to. It is okay for your best man to keep you in the dark; many bachelor parties are of the surprise variety. Just be clear with your best man about what types of activities are acceptable to you, and which ones are not. Try to do something unique and interesting where lots of your best friends and closest family can be involved.

- Don't be caught off guard if your fiancée goes on her own version of this event, the bachelorette party. Her friends will be taking her out for their own celebration of their last night of fun before she takes on the old "ball and chain" (that's you, in case you didn't know).

- The rehearsal dinner is a traditional event often held the night before the wedding. Your family usually foots the bill when they can. You can have a backyard barbecue, a semiformal dinner, or just about anything in between. This is a chance for your and the bride's families to meet each other before they are joined together by your marriage, and you can use this opportunity to give out gifts to the wedding party if you would like. This may be your best chance to make a toast, and there may be a few others. For example, your father may want a chance to be heard.

- Some couples choose to plan a gathering after the wedding reception, like an after party or a morning-after brunch. After all, when all is said and done, you don't want to feel that you and your bride were so busy speaking with well-wishers and catching up with friends and family that you didn't get a chance to celebrate your own wedding! A late-night greasy spoon, a bowling alley, or a karaoke bar are all great options, depending on the type of fun you choose. If you want to simply be alone with your new bride, that's a perfect plan, too.

- Make it a priority to take a honeymoon with your new bride, whatever shape the plans may take. This is the perfect time for a vacation, a stress-free environment for the two of you to begin your lives as a married couple. Select a trip that will be fun for both of you. So whether it's skiing or the tropics, you are already making decisions together as a couple that you are both happy with.

CHAPTER 10

Speech!

A wedding is a many-splendored thing—or maybe that's love, I don't remember. Both are multifaceted, complex things that have their moments but can still be beautiful in the end. The speeches, toasts, vows, and thank-yous that you'll run into over the course of the wedding planning can be the same way. Each one of these can affect the overall feel of the event. It will be remembered if your guests had a great time, but never received a thank-you for their gift. If the reception is on a roll and everyone is having a great time, but the best man's speech is long and rambling, or filled with off-color stories, it will change the course of the entire evening. And some nervousness is great when you're saying your vows, but you don't want to make everyone in the audience—or your BTB!—squirm in embarrassment when you open your mouth. That's why you are here for guidance, and that's why we practice these things beforehand.

Toasts

At your wedding, there will be several toasts. Some will be good; some may be bad. All, however, will be made with good intentions. If you keep in mind that everyone's heart is in the right place, then you are ready to hear what they are trying to say.

But what are *you* going to say when you give your toast at the rehearsal dinner (and maybe even at the reception)? Well, you want to thank your families and friends, tell your BTB how much you love her and how excited you are to be getting married, and basically just express your gratitude for any and all help that you received during the wedding planning process. As you've learned, it really does take a village. Now, you may feel like you're practicing for a public speaking class, but if you do not prepare, who knows what will come out of your mouth? Don't worry, the following tips will help you prepare for the big stage:

- **Know Thyself:** The classic advice from the Oracle still holds true here: Be yourself. If you are not a funnyman, then don't go up there and try to leave them in stitches. If you are not prone to quote famous poems, maybe this isn't the time to start. It's like Owen Wilson's character says in *Wedding Crashers*: It has to come from the heart.
- **There's No "I" in "Speech":** When you're practicing your speech, if you keep hearing the words "I" and "me," then it's time to revise. This speech isn't about you. As we mentioned, your speech is about your BTB, your families, and your friends who have helped you plan the wedding. Unfortunately when

we get nervous, it is easy to talk about something we know well, a.k.a. ourselves. Be kind, be insightful, be funny. Just don't make it about you.

- **Keep It Appropriate:** There are certain things that may seem funny to mention, but may only be funny if you are out having a beer with your buddies, not looking at Grandma in the front row. No mention of ex-anything, and no negativity should creep into your speech, or you may seem like a creep to those listening. If there is something you must slip into your speech, start with your original thought, bleach and lighten it about three times so it becomes *very* light-hearted in nature, and then reconsider including it once more.

See, it's really easy, right? Well, writing it may seem easy, but remembering it and giving it in front of your guests will not be so easy. So review your toast many times, have a drink (but not more than two!), and go for it. Don't worry, these are your friends and family; there will not be too many harsh critics in the crowd. And remember, you can always get with your best man and go over some of these tips, just in case, you know, you do not have total faith in his ability to prepare for his wedding toast . . .

I think you're better off going with something from the heart. Honestly.

—Owen Wilson in Wedding Crashers, on wedding toasts

Thank-Yous

We briefly discussed thank-you notes in Chapter 8, but it's so important that we have to say it again: Please don't forget to write thank-you notes to all of your guests. Even if they only gave you a spoon from your registry, they expended time, energy, and their hard-earned cash to attend and witness your wedding. So they deserve just a little of your time and a note of thanks in return. And now that you are a married, productive member of society, you cannot get by with text and e-mail, so what should you do? And when should you do it?

Grab Some Paper

That college-ruled notebook is okay, right? The one with the perforated edges that's often severely frayed and has a tear? No! This isn't good enough. If you fell into my trap, perhaps you should allow your better half to pick out the thank-you cards or notes. So put down the notebook and listen up! You can always buy thank-you cards from the store, but if you—or your fiancée—don't want to go that route, you have some options. If you are traveling somewhere of note for your honeymoon, you can grab postcards from the hotel or a cool stop on your trip. You can also always go that extra mile and turn one of your wedding photos or honeymoon photos into a batch of postcards to send gift-givers. Besides, postcards are smaller than a page from a notebook, so when you write a brief note, it still fills the page.

Keep It Simple

You don't need to go on and on endlessly expressing your gratitude unless you truly feel that way, or unless you're writing a long letter to a relative. Otherwise, keep your thank-yous short and sweet. Here, without further ado, is the secret formula for writing the best thank-you notes:

- **Drop a line:** We are going to keep it simple. Greet the person or couple. The salutation doesn't have to be extremely formal, but "What's shakin'?" doesn't work, either. Just be friendly; after all, you're sending these notes out to your friends and family. And if you cared enough to invite them to the wedding, you hopefully feel comfortable starting out your note by saying something like "Hi Aunt Ethel" or "Dear Uncle Paul."
- **Thank them for giving you the gift:** Remember, if they gave you cash or check, simply say "Thanks for your generosity." You don't need to name a specific amount. However, you do want to be specific if your guest gave you a specific gift. Yes, it can seem awkward to thank them for something on the small side, like "Thanks for the soup spoon." But it is proper. You can always thank them for "contributing to your dining room place settings."
- **Tell them about it:** Let them know what you are doing with the gift, like "The gravy boat came in handy this week when we made turkey." Don't prattle on and on. Just let them know what you have done or what plans you may have for their gift.
- **Just one more:** End the note. This can be as simple as "It was great to see you" or thanking them for traveling to your wedding.

Remember, people don't need too much detail. If they can pick up your note, say to themselves, "Hey, this is great.

They already are putting our gift to good use" and move on with their lives, then everyone will be happy. They may even be likely to give you an even better gift the next time you get married. Just kidding.

For Your Fiancée

You may feel that writing out thank-you notes falls under your BTB's jurisdiction. While this is traditionally the case, think about how stressed out you'd feel if you had to write out eighty thank-you notes on a deadline to your family and friends and help your BTB out. After all, it's in your best interest to take her stress levels down a notch. ■

Be Timely

You're exhausted. Maybe you—or your BTB—just sat through an entire bridal or Jack and Jill shower. Maybe you just got back from your honeymoon and are feeling overwhelmed trying to figure out where to put all the awesome gifts that your guests bought you for your wedding. Unfortunately, now is not the time to sink into that armchair and relax. Etiquette says that you have two weeks after a shower to send out your thank-yous. Fortunately, you have a little more time after the wedding, but not much. You may have heard that you have up to a year to get those wedding thank-yous in the mail, and while traditionally that's the timeline, you really want to get your act together a little earlier. Today, most wedding experts (including Emily Post, and who wants to cross her?) recommend that you get those thank-yous in the mail within three months after the wedding. Your guests cared enough to get you that high-end cheese grater that your BTB insisted on putting on your registry, and you need to care enough to thank them in a timely manner. So get writing!

Nuptial Knowledge

In the Mandarin culture, a statue of which animal that mates for life is given as a wedding present?

■ A duck.

Vows

The history of vows goes back a long way, back to the Anglican religion and Henry VIII. Their purpose is to establish and convey the couples' commitment and never-ending love for one another. "As long as we both shall live" and "for better and for worse" may be some of the familiar phrases that you are used to hearing. These come from the traditional vows where you repeat after the celebrant. It is time-honored, and if you think you will be nervous, you just have to repeat after the priest or official a few words at a time.

Today, many couples want to customize their wedding as much as possible. They want to "own" their wedding, to have it be one of a kind and something special that they can cherish for a long, long time. One way to do that is for you and your BTB to write and say your own vows at the ceremony. If you are going to go out on your own and write your own vows, then we are here to help. Here is what you need to do:

- Confer with your officiant to make sure there are no specific phrases that must be included in the vows.

- Talk it over with your BTB. Before you start writing, sit down with your BTB and figure out what kind of vows you both want to write. You don't want to get to the altar and find that your fiancée has written three pages of heartfelt vows while you only came up with a paragraph of (equally heartfelt, I'm sure) things to say. Also, if you want some consistency within your vows—maybe you want to end them in a similar fashion or something like that—now is the time to figure that out.

- Sit down in a place you can focus and reflect. You will need some time to gather your thoughts.

- Focus your mind on your future bride. What are some of the qualities that you love about her? What does she mean to you? What would you like to promise her, or "vow" to her, going forward? What are some special memories the two of you share (even slightly embarrassing ones)? Write all of this down.

- As for the art of eloquence, you can get on your computer and look up others' efforts in this area. Don't be afraid to quote a poem or Shakespeare if you find something that's especially meaningful and relevant.

- Now go back through all of those vows from others, through the memories the two of you share, the qualities you love about her, the promises you want to make, and the quotes from other writers if you found any. Get the best of all of that, and start to make your vows.

- Once your vows are written down, get in front of a mirror and practice early and often. And then practice some more!

See, this should be fun. Nothing says "good times" like laying your heart out there for all your guests to see. That's what all the practice is for. You should be able to recite your vows in your sleep, so you can overcome any nerves you may experience on the big day. And just as an aside, you can tell by the fact that I recommend practicing your vows that I don't think it's a good idea to write them on a napkin at a bar the night before your wedding. In a way, you are giving your bride a gift, pledging yourself to her forever, through thick and thin, fat and skinny, good times and bad. Who could ask for anything more? So plan ahead. Your BTB deserves it.

Also, even though you can recite the vows in your sleep, you may want to print out those vows and put them in the pocket of your wedding tux. Standing in front of your family and friends staring at your BTB is not the time to have a brain fart if you don't have a backup.

Get with the Wedding Program!

- Weddings are filled with many special moments, whether they be your best man's speech or a few quiet moments chatting with a grandparent. It is all about you and your bride of course, but these small pieces of interaction with your family and friends can take your wedding experience to the next level. Do your part to prepare, and have your best man prepare, for each of your turns at the microphone. Your words will touch every guest and make it a great time for them as well.

- When it is your turn to toast, be yourself. Go with your instincts and natural personality. Your toast doesn't have to sound or feel like anyone else's speech. While there is an art to giving a great toast, there is not a specific formula. Know yourself, make sure you are keeping on topic, keep it appropriate, and for good-ness' sake, practice it! Do not be afraid to check in with the best man to see how he is coming along with his. You may or may not be toasting at the rehearsal dinner, but just about every wedding has a toast from the best man.

- When it comes time to enjoy yourselves after the wedding has run its course, don't forget to send out thank-you notes. They do not need to be lengthy, just quick and polite. Try to be creative and have a little fun when tackling the burdensome project of writing thank-you notes to guests for their gifts. Purchase a size of note that will be easy to fill up. Consider using a wedding or honeymoon photo made into a card to make it personal.

- Writing your own vows is a great way to personalize your wedding, even if it is a little intimidating. Put some real thought into what makes your bride so special, and promise to be hers forever. Share a small memory you hold dear about the two of you. If your words are honest and authentic, then they will be perfect.

CHAPTER 11

What to Expect on the Big Day

The die has been cast. The months and months of planning have all come down to this moment. You and your (almost!) bride have experienced setbacks, ups and downs, great news, and bad breaks. Now it is time to bring it all home. It is not time to slip up and let things fall through the cracks though. So let's work on setting your expectations and making sure things are in good order, from the few weeks before your wedding all the way up to your big day.

Last-Minute To-Dos

Do you have your outfit? Shoes and underwear? I sure hope so! There is always a lot to do when it comes to a huge undertaking like a wedding. Look to the following list to make sure there aren't any wedding emergencies—or at least any that you and your fiancée can prevent:

- **Are You Ready?:** Did you get a haircut? Hopefully
  you did this about a week before the big day. This
  way you will have a bit of time to recover from any
  mishaps that occurred at the barber shop. Hopefully
  this wasn't the time you decided to "go for" a new
  look.
- **Double-Check:** Maybe a week beforehand is a good
  time to double-check with the vendors you are using
  for the ceremony. Hey, cake guy, you got that design?
  Everything is good? Reconfirm the time and the plan
  with each vendor so there can be no excuses.
- **Grab That Gratuity:** Many people like to tip some
  extra cash for their vendors who do an especially great
  job. If you feel this way, then get everything ready
  ahead of time. You will not want to be fumbling for
  cash in your wallet, or trying to write a check as you
  are on the dance floor. Organize yourself beforehand
  and get envelopes ready with any tips you may feel are
  appropriate. As we've previously mentioned, feel free
  to pass the tip envelopes off to your best man to hand
  out to your vendors. Why worry about another detail
  when you can pass it off to someone who won't have
  as much on his mind as you will?
- **Cash Is King:** You should probably have some cash
  on hand as well for unforeseen circumstances. Maybe
  you want the limo to make an extra stop. Maybe you
  want to tip the band to play an extra set. Maybe one
  of your vendors does an extra heroic job and you want
  to give them an extra $20. It's always good to keep a
  little extra cash around just in case something unex-
  pected, either good or bad, comes up.

- **Where Am I?:** The wedding day or weekend is a blur. We will talk about this more later. But even if you are not like the dad in *Meet the Parents* (played by Robert De Niro) where you have a minute-by-minute plan, at least write down where you are supposed to be at any given time. You should know what time you want to be at the church (or wherever the wedding will be held), when pictures are to take place, and what time you need to show up at the reception venue. As you begin to fill in these events that have a firm time element to them, you will begin to see how the day is taking shape.
- **Plan for Inclement Weather . . . and Other Acts of God:** Plan for emergencies, both big and small. It may be something as little as having a few umbrellas available for guests getting to their car after the reception, or having a sewing kit somewhere handy if you accidently pop a button off your shirt. On your wedding day, both big and little things may try to derail your grand plans, so make contingencies to keep them from becoming a huge headache.

Who knew there was so much to do for a wedding that you have been planning for months? Just when you thought it was safe, there is more to think about. At some point, there is nothing left that can be done, and you simply have to hope you have got it all covered. If you don't have it all covered, then you will have to simply laugh and make the best of it because you're getting close to your wedding day . . .

For Your Fiancée

You may notice your BTB starting to get pretty anxious (like bridezilla-anxious) in the days and weeks leading up to the wedding. Try to help her calm down by planning a special date (maybe to the place you went on your first date or to her favorite restaurant) that makes her feel loved and appreciated. The time away may help her feel refreshed and more able to handle the last-minute wedding planning details—which you should offer to help out with as well, by the way. ■

What to Expect

You've spent months planning and rehashing every last detail of your wedding with your BTB, and now the planning is coming to a close and it's time to actually celebrate. You do have some things to take care of in the day or two leading up your wedding, but what will actually happen the day of? How will the ceremony go down? What will you do the day before when every last tiny bow has been tied (thank God!), your out-of-town guests have arrived, and every last detail has been attended to? What you should do is have fun! Here's some info on what you should expect, so just relax and enjoy the ride!

The Day Before

The day before your wedding, you will wake up, fully knowing that the wedding is tomorrow. But it will not really feel like it is going to happen. You and your BTB have talked about it endlessly, planned for it (endlessly), and thought about it all the time. But like two senior citizens in the sack together, nothing's actually happened. But that's all about to change. Here's some info on what you'll end up doing the day before your wedding.

The Boys Are Back in Town

When you wake up in the morning, chances are good that you'll stretch, check your phone, and see that you have some texts and messages from friends who are on their way. The calls and texts will likely pick up as the day progresses, and you'll probably want to get together with some of your friends who are in town for tomorrow's big day. As you grab some lunch with your groomsmen, be prepared to field some questions from your friends like: What's on the menu at the rehearsal dinner? Where is everyone going out tonight? Hey, what is the story with that cute bridesmaid? At this point, you may be beginning to feel like this is real.

The Ceremony Rehearsal

We went over the ceremony rehearsal in detail in Chapter 9, but planning it and doing it can be two different things. This is when you start to picture what your ceremony location will look like the day of your wedding. Seeing the venue, with your officiant directing traffic and having everyone practice where to stand and when to go, is all shadowed by the moment when your bride makes her grand entrance. There's a good chance that you'll start to get goose bumps. You can actually see her in her dress. The excitement (and a bit of nerves) builds up inside you.

Keep in mind that, as we discussed, you and your BTB may have chosen to have the rehearsal and rehearsal dinner a little earlier in the week. If this is the case, that's great! It just gives you more time to relax, enjoy the company of your guests, and get ready to get married.

The Rehearsal Dinner

After you practice getting married, you'll likely proceed to the rehearsal dinner. Maybe you picked the restaurant where you had your first date. Either way, your reserved room is ready, and the guests flood in. "Guests" is too strong of a word, as they are grandparents, uncles, aunts, and of course your groomsmen. Her family is there as well. You can see the families coming together, slowly at first, but it is definitely happening. They are putting their best foot forward, trying to smooth over their rough edges, out of their respective love for each of you. Two glasses of wine and a full meal later, you realize it is time for you to give your toast. It goes off (almost) without a hitch. Then your dad is up, and does a fabulous and gracious toast. He makes it look so easy!

The Night Before

As the night wraps up, try and grab a few precious moments with your parents. They probably want to tell you how proud they are of you, and how bright your future is. Or maybe they just want to ask you when they can expect to get some grandchildren. At this point, it's okay to roll your eyes and head off to meet some out-of-town friends. A few drinks, a few laughs, and you realize you are pretty much surrounded by everyone you care about. It is a pretty awesome feeling.

Now as you're out having fun with your friends, keep in mind that you're getting married tomorrow—and you don't want to spend a day that you've spent forever planning tired, cranky, or worse, hung-over. And you don't want to face your bride at the altar smelling of alcohol. So pack it in early and say no to those last few drinks. Trust me on this one.

For Your Fiancée

It's tradition for couples to spend the night before the wedding apart from each other. Many brides will spend the night at their parents' house with their bridesmaids, leaving you to your own devices. Enjoy the quiet, because you'll have someone in bed next to you every night for the rest of your life. But just because you're apart doesn't mean you shouldn't tell your BTB how much you love her and how you're thinking about her, so send her a text message or slip a note into her purse that she can only open once you've said your goodnights. ∎

The Ceremony

"Dearly Beloved, we are gathered here today . . ."

This is a classic part of many ceremonies, and it will be one of the first things you hear if you are taking part in a traditional ceremony. But what will that day actually be like? I am here to offer a few observations gathered from grooms I know to give you a little insight into what lies ahead of you:

The Morning Of . . .

You will wake up on the big day with a fresh perspective—and a fresh case of nerves. Try to keep yourself busy by starting the day off with a quick brunch with your family. There will likely be a quiet buzz in the room about the impending nuptials, and if you and your bride have decided to keep tradition, you won't see her until the wedding. It's okay to wonder what she is doing and to text her to let her know how excited you are.

After brunch, it's time for you and your groomsmen to start getting ready and head to the ceremony venue. But before you head into the limo, you have some things to do:

- **Put On Your Tux:** Most grooms get dressed before they leave for the ceremony. After all, if you're wearing it, you can't leave it behind, right? If you do plan to get dressed at the ceremony venue, double- and triple-check that you and your groomsmen have everything you need. You don't want to get to the venue and find out that you've forgotten your shoes or that your best man forgot his suit jacket.

- **Gather Up Your Stuff:** You don't have a lot to remember, but what you do have to bring with you is important. Make sure you have the tip envelopes to give to your vendors (or make sure your best man has them—seriously, double-check with him). Make sure you have your bag packed to bring to wherever you and your BTB are spending your first night. And, even if you forget everything else, make sure you have your BTB's wedding band.

Once you get this stuff done, it's time to pile into the van or car or limo or whatever it is that's getting you and your groomsmen to the ceremony.

Don't be afraid if you get a few calls about some things that may not be going quite right. The truth is, everything won't go exactly the way you imagined/planned it. At this point, what really matters is that you don't sweat the small stuff. After all, you're getting married; who cares if the photographer is running late? Hopefully, someone in your wedding party (this is where the best man starts to come in really handy) will take care of any issues that come up.

Once you get to the ceremony venue, you'll likely find yourself in a groom's holding room, where you and your groomsmen hang out and wait for the show to start. If you weren't nervous before, you'll probably start to feel those butterflies now. So take the time to run over everything with your groomsmen again: who stands where, does your best man still have the ring, etc. Once you're sure you have all your ducks in a row, feel free to pass around a bottle of peppermint schnapps, say a quick prayer together, and head out to get married.

Every bride is beautiful. It's like newborn babies or puppies. They can't help it.

—Emme Rollins, author

On with the Show

Once the ceremony begins, you'll make your entrance and look out into the crowd. At this point, you'll probably feel excited and maybe even slightly dizzy. Don't be afraid if things seem to drag for a minute; if your fiancée is like most brides, she's probably the one holding things up. It doesn't mean that she won't show up at the altar.

Once your BTB starts to walk down the aisle, things are going to start moving really fast—and yet you might feel like they're moving in slow motion. This is a good thing. Savor these moments! And remember to breathe as you read your vows and say "I do." No one wants to see the groom hyperventilate at the front of the church or hall. Once you hear your officiant say "I now pronounce you man and wife," you're good to go! Don't hesitate to swoop in for that kiss. It's what you've been waiting for, and it is probably the best kiss you can ever remember. Makes all that stress and planning worth it, right? Now that the official business is over, it's time to party. So on to the reception!

Nuptial Knowledge

Why, in the traditional wedding ceremony, does the bride always stand on the left side?

■ This is for the groom to have easy access to draw his sword and defend his claim to his bride against jealous suitors. I guess today it would allow you a quick pivot to bring a right-handed haymaker to any guys horning in on your woman.

The Reception

Once you've tied the knot, the reception is just crazy. You are bombarded by all sorts of well-wishers who just want a few moments with the happy couple. Once you enter the reception, all bets are off. The newlyweds often sit up front at their own special table. The constant clinking of glasses is the universal sign for the two of you to kiss. It will probably happen a million and one times. At some point the stress and exhaustion catch up with you, and you want to kick back and have a good time. But not so fast! You still have duties to perform. Let's look at a typical reception schedule:

- Your guests arrive before you and your bride. It's often time for cocktail hour. This is guests mingling, and drinking. You may be driving around in the limo with the wedding party or taking photos.
- The happy couple makes their grand entrance. The crowd goes wild.

- It's time for dinner, whatever form it is taking. Usually there is an announcement to let everyone know to quit gabbing and head to their seats.
- Shortly after dinner gets started, it is time for the toasts. Hopefully the best man is ready to go with a properly prepared speech. Let's hope he did not over-indulge and doesn't attempt to "improve" his speech with some off-color humor or a "mic drop."
- The first dance is announced. This will have already been predetermined ahead of time, including which song is played, and if anyone will be joining you on the dance floor. Some couples break out their ball-room moves they have practiced and want the floor to themselves; other times, after a minute or two, the parents and wedding parties will get out there.
- If your bride and her dad are doing a dance, this is when it will happen. The DJ or band will announce the dance and ask your bride and her dad to head out to the dance floor. Prepare for lots of applause and a few teary eyes.
- Some grooms choose to dance with their mothers at this point. If this is something you've chosen to do, the DJ or band will again announce the dance and ask you and your mom to head out to the floor.
- Everybody on the dance floor. There is an amazing phenomenon that often occurs at the reception. Early on, the dance floor is often a little empty. As the evening gets later, more and more dancing goes on. I'm sure it has nothing to do with the amount of alcohol consumed . . .
- Time for a break now that everyone is loosened up. It's likely that you and your new bride are a tiny bit

tipsy at this point, but you still have some responsibilities to take care of before your wedding night
starts. Remember that cake you tasted and ordered
and topped? Well, it's time to cut it. And make sure
you prepare yourself for the deluge of photo-taking
that accompanies this special moment. Seriously, it's
like you're being stalked by paparazzi, but you'll
appreciate it when it's time to sit down and look at
the photos. Typically, the cake is served with champagne and/or coffee. This is so that group "A," if you
will, can downshift with coffee, cake, and water if
needed and group "B," which is often lead by your
oldest friends who look ready to drink the bar dry, can
continue to do so.

- Okay, you have goofed off enough. It's time to wrap
up your official duties and get this show on the road.
It's time for the bouquet toss and the garter fling. The
bride tosses her bouquet to a crowd of single ladies
gathered for just such an event. Then you remove the
garter from your bride's leg and fling it into a crowd
of single guys. The custom says the recipient of these
items will be the next to get married.

- The announcement is made that you and the bride
will be leaving. People used to throw rice, but now
anything goes—confetti, a few doves—whatever you
deem necessary to get you on your way.

- Depending on the lateness of the hour, people may
linger at the reception, hoping a party breaks out. If
you've organized an after party (as discussed in Chapter 9), this is the time to move people out of the reception hall to that event.

- At this point, you and your bride should now be on your way to somewhere fun, maybe the after party or maybe one night at a hotel before going to the airport to begin your honeymoon. Either way, it's time to start out what will hopefully be your long, happy marriage together!

Your reception schedule may vary wildly from this one; it all depends on how you and your fiancée (now bride) have planned it. But even if that's true, hopefully this gives you an idea of just how crazy and busy the day can be. Between all of these scheduled events at the reception, you will start but never finish 100 conversations, each one with someone important in your life. You'll realize that you forgot to do something that originally felt very important, and you won't give a damn. And you'll have a great time dancing and celebrating with your friends, family, and bride. But since the day is so busy, there are some things that you should really slow down and make sure you do at your own wedding:

Remember to Dance

You are there to celebrate this important occasion, whether it is for you or someone you know. There are better ways to celebrate than standing on the sidelines like a schmo or drinking your way through the reception while getting to know the bartender really well. You are there to be with family and friends, so even if your dance moves are a little unorthodox, go ahead and get on the dance floor. If you are really nervous about that first dance, don't hesitate to sign up for a few lessons ahead of time. Even learning the basics for that first dance will impress your guests and, more importantly, your bride. Imagine yourself gliding across the floor in that first dance while your friends look on, impressed.

Talk to Your Family . . .

Spend a few minutes with gramps: There are bound to be some family members or guests from the older generation at your wedding. Make sure you grab them and spend a few minutes with them. Whether they share a simple story with you, or tell you the key to their forty years of marriage, you just might learn something from them. Besides, old people are funny.

But Don't Talk Too Much

Tons of newly married couples spend so much time making the rounds to all of the tables, talking to all of their guests, that they never really get a chance to enjoy their own wedding. Don't let this be you! Yes, you want to socialize with your guests, but you've spent months planning this party and you need to enjoy it, too. So say a few words to Aunt Ethel and Grandma and then get out on the dance floor!

Eat Your Meal

This may sound funny, but make sure you actually eat your meal at the reception when it's served to you. Yes, you want to talk to everyone and celebrate, but this is one time where you and your BTB really need to hunker down and be selfish. There's a good chance that one—or both—of you were too nervous to eat breakfast this morning, and you're not going to make it through all of the champagne toasts without something in your stomach. And you paid all that money for your meal, so don't let it go to waste!

For Your Fiancée

Your wedding day will go by in a flash, so you need to cherish those quiet moments with your bride when you can. Kiss her in the limo. Hold her hand as you eat your meal (seriously, make sure you eat it!). Tell her how much you love her in the moments you have alone before you're announced at the reception. Your bride will remember her wedding day forever, and making those small moments count will go a long way. ■

Just Have Fun

Just remember that no matter how stressful or crazy your wedding day is or how totally drained you feel the next day, it is an awesome event that will leave you very happy when you wake up the next day, wherever that is, next to your new wife. Enjoy every second of it because it will go by in the blink of an eye. This is where that videographer will come in handy! But, really, make sure that you cherish your wedding day. It's worth the work and it's a time you'll remember forever. Congratulations!

Nuptial Knowledge

True or False: The throwing of the bride's garter and bouquet is a modification of the ancient tradition of taking a piece of the bride's dress for good luck.

■ True. It used to be good luck to steal a piece of the bride's dress, and people used to sneak into the couple's bedroom to do so. That's pretty creepy, so today the groom throws the garter to ensure some privacy on his wedding night.

Get with the Wedding Program!

- Just when you thought you were done, there is still a lot more to do. Double-checking with all of the vendors you have hired about a week before the wedding is always a good idea.

- You will want to think about making tip envelopes for the vendors. It is common practice to give them a tip if they do an especially great job at your wedding, and you don't want to be scrambling during the reception to make this happen.

- You may want to carry a little extra spending cash with you to the wedding and reception. You never know what complications may arise, and having some extra cash with you will help you be prepared to solve some of those little unforeseen emergencies.

- Even if you are not a natural planner, you will want to sketch out a general overview of all the wedding-related events and the overall schedule. If nothing else, it will give you a general picture of how everything holds together and if you have any conflicts or problems creeping into your schedule. You may want to spend a few minutes to plan for inclement weather like heavy rain and consider how it may affect your proceedings. Your plan may be as complicated as having an indoor backup for your outdoor wedding, or as simple as providing umbrellas for guests to get to their cars.

- Even though you are ready to kick back after the ceremony ends, the reception has a schedule as well. The grand entrance, the reception line, the cake cutting: these are all things that will happen on some sort of schedule. Don't forget to kiss when everyone clinks their fork to their glass.

After the Dust Settles

Congratulations! You and your bride, with a little help along the way, successfully planned the perfect wedding. The invites made it out on time, and your registry was made. The cakes were mouthwatering, the church was stately, and the flowers were beautiful. All of the little details were taken care of, and you and your bride dealt with any problems that came up with confidence and grace. The ceremony ran smoothly. The "I dos" have all been said, and the reception was historic. It was a great wedding by all accounts.

Now it's time to begin your lives as a married couple. Whether or not you have lived together, or are taking the old-school approach where this is your first time sharing a living space, it's time to start the beginning of the rest of your lives as husband and wife. Here at *Dude* headquarters, we root for every couple to end up happy, and as the two of you better understand each other, your marriage will grow stronger with each passing day. That is the goal, though it is not always easy. To make it easier moving forward, keep the following in mind:

- Remember that nobody is perfect; you will hurt your wife's feelings at some point, and she will do the same to you. Forgive and move on.
- Just as your interests, hobbies, and attitudes continually evolve, so must your marriage; both you and your wife must change and evolve while keeping the love between the two of you alive.
- As the years pass, don't take each other for granted. Put the effort into your marriage and take good care of yourself as well.
- Be nice to each other. Don't underestimate the power of a positive or negative attitude. Nagging, making fun of your spouse, or being negative about her to someone else is hurtful. Don't do it.

You two are taking a leap of faith together. You have met a person so special that you have decided it is worth the risk. The best advice that you can take is to embrace changes in your lives as they come. When you are experiencing good times, enjoy them to the fullest. When times are tough, hang in there.

And now that the dust from your wedding and honeymoon has settled, it is time to get started on having the time of your lives together. Congratulations and enjoy the ride!

The Best Wedding Movies of All Time. Period!

I have always wanted to be a movie critic. I once sent a review of *Dead Man Walking* in to the *Atlanta Journal-Constitution*. Those were my first (unpaid) words to appear in print. And, as an avid movie watcher, I have learned two things about movies. First, movies mirror real life, or at least try to. The best ones do it in a meaningful, relatable way, with characters you care about. The second thing I have learned is that movies sometimes show us a world in which things happen the way we wish life would turn out. This is no different in the many, many movies that have been made about weddings and the craziness that comes with them.

So in the months leading up to your wedding, you and your fiancée may want to kick back, relax, and watch some wedding movies. It will be a fun way for the two of you to laugh (or cry) about the wedding process that has taken over your lives. Each one has a sliver of truth to it, something relatable, and a thing or two you can take from it. So without further ado, here are the top ten wedding movies reviewed by your friendly neighborhood movie critic.

- *Father of the Bride*: Watching the parents of the soon-to-be happy couple meet (awkwardly) and watching George go from panic to a full-on conniption should bring chuckles out of both of you.
- *My Best Friend's Wedding*: We should all be so lucky as to have Cameron Diaz and Julia Roberts fighting over us!
- *Four Weddings and a Funeral*: This film, which received an Academy Award nomination for Best Picture, will be fun for both of you.
- *Serendipity*: This quirky movie about love and fate is one of my favorites.
- *Made of Honor*: In this film, a man tries to be the maid of honor. It's fun and lighthearted.
- *Bridesmaids*: This is like an all-girl version of *The Hangover*.
- *The Wedding Date*: Julia Roberts hires a handsome man to be her wedding date.
- *Wedding Crashers*: If adult humor is not your cup of tea, maybe you should skip this one, because jokes about sexual exploits and debauchery are the main theme.
- *Sweet Home Alabama*: This one is my wife's all-time favorite, so it had to make the list.
- *The Hangover*: The Vegas bachelor party gone horribly wrong!

So there you go. Ten wedding-themed movies of varying overall quality, but each with some great hooks to keep you entertained for a few hours. By far and away, this type of movie is dominated by the romantic comedy, but I included a few regular comedies as well for your viewing pleasure. I could do an "honorable mention" section of movies here a mile long, but I won't. I hope this list will guide you toward a method of bringing a few hours of lighthearted relaxation to you and your BTB in the months leading up to your big day.

INDEX

About the Author

John Pfeiffer has been through it all—from buying the ring (she still gets compliments) to successful negotiations to getting his own groom's cake (complete with Superman logo, of course). He has been a groomsman, best man (didn't even lose the ring), and now a husband for more than a decade. He's also the author of *Dude, You're Gonna Be a Dad!* and *Dude, You're a Dad!* John lives in the suburbs of Atlanta, GA, with his wife and three children.